Fruit of the Spirit

Reflections on Growing in Christ

Mel Eyeons

Published by Eltisley Books

ISBN: 978-1-9162689-0-6

A CIP record for this book is available from the British Library

See page 160 for further copyright acknowledgements

Editor Helen Jones

Page layout and cover design Helen Jones

Cover photograph Henri Guérin

Contents

INTRODUCTION

*By contrast, the fruit of the Spirit is love, joy, peace,
patience, kindness, generosity, faithfulness, gentleness,
and self-control. There is no law against such things.*

Galatians 5.22-23 (NRSVA)

About me

I'm a Licensed Lay Minister (also known as a Reader) in
the Church of England, living in Cambridgeshire with my
husband, three gerbils and some hens. My ministry mainly
involves preaching, leading services, doing radio talks, blog-
ging, and now writing this book. I have a degree in theology
and I'm doing an MA in church history as I believe there's
always more to learn about God, life, faith and the church.

Outside the church I work freelance as a proofreader for
university students in Cambridge who have learning difficulties such as dyslexia. Before I started that I worked for many
years in university libraries.

I also enjoy playing the clarinet and reading, and I try to
keep fit through running.

This book arises in many ways from my own journey
through life and faith. Having gone through an abusive
childhood I have experienced difficulties such as anxiety and
depression. Working through my past and what it means to
have faith in these circumstances has been challenging at
times, but I've been greatly helped by the kindness, patience
and wisdom of fellow-Christians, including my friends and
my husband, as well as by going to therapy. So, many of
the thoughts in this book arise from what I've learned along

the way from others as well as my own understanding and experiences.

If you would like to read more of what I have written on different subjects you can follow me at:

www.thoughtsfromareader.com

https://www.facebook.com/thoughtfulLLM/

How this book works

This book contains a series of reflections on the fruit of the Spirit as referred to by Paul in the verses above.

The aim is to explore the fruit of the Spirit by looking at different themes that arise from each of its aspects and considering how they might affect our lives, actions, thinking and relationships today.

The reflections build on the idea of each part of the fruit with thoughts springing from the starting point of Galatians and covering our relationships with God, others, ourselves and the wider world.

The book contains 27 reflections covering different aspects of the fruit of the Sprit, grouped into three main sections as:

1 Love, kindness & generosity

2 Joy, peace & self-control

3 Patience, gentleness & faithfulness.

Then there is a final reflection which summarises the fruit of the Spirit as a whole.

Therefore, you could cover all the reflections over four weeks or dip in and out as and when you like – each one can be read on its own without having to read all the others.

After each reflection there are also suggestions for exploration and prayer which you might want to consider in order to go more deeply or find your own ways to work with the Spirit to develop the fruit in your life.

I've tried to include a range of different kinds of activities to appeal to different styles of learning and prayer, as well as books and online resources.

There's also a list of books and other resources at the end of this book, including ones that I refer to during this book, should you want to explore more widely.

Background to Paul's letter to the Galatians

This letter was probably written about AD 49 to a group of churches in the Roman Empire's province of Galatia, in modern-day central Turkey. Paul wrote it at a time when an argument had arisen between Jewish and non-Jewish followers of Jesus. The Jewish followers believed that all followers should be circumcised and follow Jewish law.

Paul, however, was horrified at this idea. He, despite being Jewish himself, believed firmly that salvation is a gift joyfully and freely given by God to all who believe – whether Jewish or not. So, faith is the basis of life and salvation, with love the only law under which people must live. And Paul wrote this very strongly worded letter, to assert the freedom of Christ's followers.

What is the fruit of the Spirit?

> *People, in Paul's view, are not to be judged by their performance but on what they are and have received from Christ.*
>
> *Oxford Dictionary of the Bible*

So it is that Paul talks about the fruit of the Spirit as something that grows in us as we begin to live our new life in Christ through faith, and as we begin to walk according to the Spirit rather than the flesh. The flesh isn't necessarily about physical failings and weaknesses but refers to humanity apart from God. The fruit of the Spirit refers to positive qualities and characteristics that come from living a life aligned with God.

However, developing the fruit of the Spirit isn't something that happens if we just put enough effort into acting in the right way. After all, in human relationships, if you suspect that someone is giving you a gift because they've decided that they have to act generously, and not because they really want to, then the giving becomes less a source of happiness and more a slightly awkward encounter between two people. So, generosity and all the other aspects of the fruit need to come from within, to be part of our character and motivations.

Neither, though, is the fruit of the Sprit something that happens automatically while we get on with our everyday lives. It's something that we have a role in as well, as we try to cooperate with God's work within us, to make sure we are open to the Spirit's promptings. We need to be set on becoming the people God wants us to be and opening our hands to receiving God's gifts to us.

And so this book sets out to explore some ways in which we might be able to work with God to help increase the fruit of the Spirit within us.

As Paul says a few verses later in this chapter of Galatians:

If we live by the Spirit, let us also be guided by the Spirit.

Galatians 5.25 (NRSVA)

LOVE, KINDNESS AND GENEROSITY

In this part of the book I consider love, kindness and generosity (or goodness) as three aspects of the fruit of the Spirit which seem to overlap and support each other. Love which takes no action, performs no kind acts and doesn't result in goodness and generosity towards others is of no use, for the love that the Bible calls us to is living and active. So:

> *Little children, let us love, not in word or speech, but in truth and action.*
>
> 1 John 3.18 (NRSVA)

On the other hand, the Bible also teaches us that love is the fundamental thing that should underlie all our actions. Love gives all our actions value and should be our primary motivator.

> *If I speak in the tongues of mortals and of angels, but do not have love, I am a noisy gong or a clanging cymbal. And if I have prophetic powers, and understand all mysteries and all knowledge, and if I have all faith, so as to remove mountains, but do not have love, I am nothing. If I give away all my possessions, and if I hand over my body so that I may boast, but do not have love, I gain nothing.*
>
> 1 Corinthians 13.1-3 (NRSVA)

So there's an interdependence, an interweaving, between love and action, which we need to have, informing and underpinning our lives and faith.

Love

Loved by God

Varieties of love

English has a problem with love.

I can tell you that I love chocolate ice cream or another human being or even God himself with just one word, and there's no way just from that word in which you can tell what kind of love I'm talking about.

There's no subtlety in it.

We must assume that the person we're talking to knows what we mean and the kind of love we feel when we say that we love someone or something.

Paul, though, writing in Greek, didn't face this difficulty because he had four words to choose from when he talked about love in his letter to the Galatians.

He could have talked about *eros* – passionate, sensual, romantic love. This is the love celebrated and wept over in many novels, films and songs. There's even a statue in Piccadilly Circus popularly thought to be of Eros, the Greek god of love.

He could have mentioned *philia* – the friendship or affection existing between friends with common values, interests or activities. This doesn't appear in so many dramatic stories and heartfelt songs but it's the basis of our happiness, contentment and feeling of security when we're with people we've known for years and with whom we don't feel the need to put up a front or pretend to be someone else.

There was also *storgē* – the bond of empathy. This is about familiarity, family members or other people we've bonded with through chance and circumstance. One example is the natural love and affection found between parent and child, when all goes well in family relationships.

Paul chose *agapē* though – unconditional, unselfish and sacrificial love – the love which continues regardless of circumstances and which agrees with Shakespeare's declaration that

> *Love is not love / Which alters when it alteration finds*

> *Sonnet 116*

This is the love that God delights to show us. As the Bible tells us,

> *In this is love, not that we loved God but that he loved us and sent his Son to be the atoning sacrifice for our sins.*

> *1 John 4.10 (NRSVA)*

God takes the initiative in loving each person and making that love always available, whether we respond to it or not. God gives his own self to rescue us from the consequences of our own wrongdoing and to stand with us in all our suffering – not out of duty or a grudging agreement to help us out but because he loves us.

It's both the simplest and most difficult of things to understand – that God should love us, as we are, with no conditions, but just because he is love. If we want to understand more of God, we must start by understanding that his whole nature and purpose is to love, and for this we can turn to people like Julian of Norwich.

Julian of Norwich

We don't know what Julian of Norwich's real name was but we do know that she was born in 1342 and lived until around 1416. She was an anchoress, someone who withdrew from everyday life for religious purposes. She would have lived in a cell attached to a church and the name we know her by comes from that church. She would have spent time in activities like prayer, contemplation, embroidery and writing, and offering prayers and advice for visitors.

Many of these visitors, and presumably Julian herself, knew a lot of hardship and pain for this was a difficult time of economic suffering, war and the Plague. Death was a constant presence in people's lives and so it's unsurprising that death and suffering were major elements of spirituality at that time. These themes come up in Julian's writings but she also focuses on the closeness and goodness of God.

On the 8th May 1373, at the age of 30, Julian received a series of 16 visions while lying on what she thought was her deathbed. This series of visions showed her that God surrounds us in love and doesn't blame or judge, and led to her producing *Revelations of Divine Love*.

She in fact wrote two versions of this: a short one immediately after her visions and a longer one after spending more time meditating on their meaning.

Julian shows us a vision of God in which there's always compassion and love, and where wrath lies in us and not in God, who aims to defuse our wrath with his love. She also, in a way which sounds remarkably modern to our ears, talks about motherhood to describe God's care for us and refers to Jesus as 'Mother'.

> *What, do you wish to know your Lord's meaning in this thing? Know it well, love was his meaning. Who reveals it to you? Love. What did he reveal you? Love. Why does he reveal it to you? For Love.*
>
> *Julian of Norwich, Revelations of Divine Love*

Everything that God does is out of love.

Everything that God plans is out of love.

And every time God speaks to us it is out of love.

This isn't always obvious, especially when we see bad news on our TV screens and on the internet, with a media industry devoted to bringing us the worst of humanity. It can be even harder when we go through difficult times or see a loved one suffering. Such things are often a mystery to us and have been throughout the history of faith.

For now, though, if things are hard, perhaps we can hold on to these words, which I have found helpful when going through times of depression:

> *When you pass through the waters, I will be with you;*
> *and through the rivers, they shall not overwhelm you;*
> *when you walk through fire you shall not be burned,*
> *and the flame shall not consume you.*

Isaiah 43.2 (NRSVA)

These are not words offering us easy answers but they do tell us that God's love doesn't let us go through difficulties alone but walks through the suffering with us – as Julian of Norwich – along with millions of Christians before and since, have found.

Suggestions for exploration and prayer

• Read Julian of Norwich's *Revelations of Divine Love* (translations in modern English are available) or a book of reflections based on them. One such book which I have found helpful is *Making All Things Well: Finding Spiritual*

Strength with Julian of Norwich by Isobel de Gruchy (Canterbury Press, 2012).

- The good things in our lives are blessings from God and signs of his love. Cut out some heart-shaped pieces of red paper and write on them the good things in your life (they can be basic things like food and shelter, big things like recovery from a serious illness or anything in-between). Stick them up somewhere you can see them to remind you that God loves you. You could also make them into flowers by adding green stalks and leaves.

- At the end of each day write down in a journal the good things and the triumphs that have happened – no matter how small – and use this as a reminder of God's love for you.

- Find or make/draw a cross and, sitting quietly in front of it, write down on Post-it notes all the things you are worried about, the things you have done wrong which are a burden to you, your hurts and fears, anything that you want to bring to a loving God. Stick them onto the cross as a sign of giving them to God and receiving his love in return.

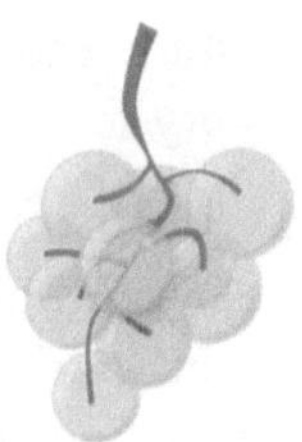

Honest love

If we know that God loves us, our next step may be to wonder how we can respond to that love. First of all, we need to really take hold of his love and let it soak into us – body, mind, heart and soul. It's easy to put up a wall to keep God out.

Am I good enough?

The wall can be built from thoughts like 'God says he loves everyone but he's angry with me because I sin or fail or think bad thoughts or forget to pray.'

David, the king of Israel, a great hero of faith, was also a murderer and an adulterer (2 Samuel 11). And yet he was still loved and God still chose him to be on the ancestral line that leads directly to Jesus.

Or we might think that we aren't the right kind of person for God because we don't have the right personality traits or abilities to be properly loved and accepted.

But think of Moses. We remember him as a bold leader who stood up to Pharaoh and led Israel across the wilderness, someone who met with God and passed on his commandments. He was a judge, a prophet, a liberator. Yet when God first spoke to Moses, this future leader and prophet was a scared shepherd with a history of violence (Exodus 2).

He felt he wasn't up to the job, that he couldn't speak properly, that someone, anyone, else would be better than him. So he poured out his fears and insecurities and God heard him, loved him, helped him and continued to have faith in him.

There's a story about an old stone well and two water pots. One was beautifully decorated and new-looking, while the other was old and cracked. No one wanted to use the old cracked pot except for a girl who came every day and chose it over the other one.

One day the pot asked the girl why she kept using it when it couldn't hold water very well. The girl took the pot down the path they travelled every day and showed it a row of wild-flowers that had bloomed there because of the water that the pot had been dripping. 'This is why,' she said.

Just like that pot, we can all be of use to God, and we can all produce beautiful things, even if we feel more like the old cracked pot than the beautiful new one.

Fear, worry and anger

Or our wall might be built from fear, worry or anger with God. This might be over the circumstances of our lives, the things that aren't fair, our deep-seated wounds, or watching the suffering and heartache of others. That's OK too. God is the safe place where we can shout, scream, cry and be however we want to be.

There's no need to pretend with God, put on a good front or be polite. God can take everything we want to throw at him and more. As long as we're communicating, there's hope.

It's when we stop having anything to do with God at all that the relationship is in danger.

We don't have to use words if they're too difficult or not what we want to use, for there are other ways to be with God (see suggestions at the end of this reflection).

The Bible also gives us examples of people who raged, shouted, wept and blamed God but he never let go of them. The Psalms, for example, are full of pretty much every human emotion, including anger with God:

How long, O LORD? Will you forget me forever?
How long will you hide your face from me?
How long must I bear pain in my soul,
and have sorrow in my heart all day long?
How long shall my enemy be exalted over me?

Psalm 13.1-2 (NRSVA)

But there's also the example of Job, who spends a lot of time being angry at God and, rather than being condemned, is declared righteous.

Unstoppable love

The thoughts that build a wall between us and God aren't true.

God loves each one of us, despite our sins, bad days and forgetfulness, and despite our quirks and weaknesses. He loves us with full acceptance that these things are part of who and where we are. So, we can come to him in prayer and worship knowing that we have nothing to worry about.

We can't stop God loving us any more than we can stop the sea being wet or the sun rising in the morning, and we can't limit, block or stop his full, open and generous love for us.

For I am convinced that neither death, nor life, nor angels, nor rulers, nor things present, nor things to come, nor powers, nor height, nor depth, nor anything else in all creation, will be able to separate us from the love of God in Christ Jesus our Lord.

Romans 8.38-39 (NRSVA)

And it's as we allow that love to sink in to us, as we open

ourselves up, openly bringing our anger and hurt, our fears and insecurities to God, that we find a change. We find healing and freedom in our relationship with God, and we find that this begins to overflow into our relationships with others.

As we become secure in our identity as loved children, with needs and flaws but also talents and abilities, we find new ways of relating to others that are less based on competition and envy and more based on how we can all be more open, honest and loving to another.

This won't happen overnight; it's a lifetime's work, but little by little we can begin to move towards being more rooted in being loved by God, loving him and loving one another.

Suggestions for exploration and prayer

- Try placing candles in a tray of water to represent your prayers about sorrow and suffering in the middle of tears, and reflect on a psalm such as Psalm 126.

- At difficult times try to see if there are any points of light: a helpful friend or loved one, a moment of joy or happiness, a comforting pet, the beauty of nature. In such things we can find God alongside us.

- Quiet meditation can be helpful for getting a sense of God's presence in your life, either silent or guided by someone else, and it has a long history in the Christian faith. A good app if you like technology is *Insight Timer*, which has thousands of different kinds of meditations, including some which are specifically Christian, some which come from other faiths, and many which are entirely secular. It will also allow you to set a timer and just sit quietly for a set amount of time.

- A good book on mindfulness meditation for Christians is *How to be a Mindful Christian: 40 Simple Spiritual Practices* by Sally Welch (Canterbury Press, 2016).

- Another helpful book if you want to think more about suffering and sorrow is *Seeing in the Dark: Pastoral Perspectives on Suffering from the Christian Spiritual Tradition* by Christopher Chapman (Canterbury Press, 2013).

- Music can be a good way to draw closer to God, whether it's listening, singing or playing an instrument. Find a kind of music that works for you.

- Start to consider your own gifts, talents and skills (we all have some) and how you might be able to use them to help others, if you're not doing so already. But don't wear yourself out by trying to do too much. It doesn't all depend on any one person.

- If things are very bad and nothing seems to help, consider seeing your GP or a therapist: there's no shame in asking for extra help.

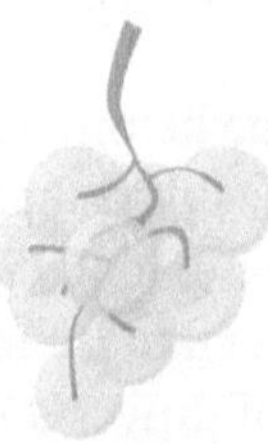

Love of self

Why we need to love ourselves

Us Christians need to do a better job of loving ourselves.

I know, it sounds all wrong, but bear with me. As Christians we rightly talk a lot about loving God and others, putting them first, not being selfish or self-centred. But how often do we hear about the need to love ourselves?

There's a strong tendency to think that the 'best' Christians are the ones who work long hours for others and never stop to think about themselves. But what happens when the long hours and lack of rest, with constant giving and never taking, and the relentless driving of ourselves, go on for too long?

What happens is that we start to show the signs of burnout: stress, depression, lack of sleep, spiritual dryness, lack of motivation, feelings of isolation, becoming more vulnerable to temptation and feeling detached from others.

None of these things help us to love others – in fact they can have the opposite effect, causing us to be too wrapped up in our difficulties to find the mental space or energy to care about other people.

Why do we drive ourselves?

There are many reasons why we might drive ourselves in this way.

We might want to cover up some needs or emptiness of our own with busyness or good deeds or to gain approval from others.

We can even get caught up in the idea that God wants us to think of ourselves as terrible sinners, worthless and dirty, not worthy of kindness, compassion or respect, while giving ourselves in love to others. It's as if everyone deserves love and kindness except us. We dress neglecting ourselves up in piety and give it an air of holiness, as if it somehow makes us more acceptable.

But stop. This can't be right.

Self-centredness and selfishness are wrong and unattractive traits but that's not what I'm talking about here. This isn't a call to enthrone the self and make your own will and desires the most important thing in the world. This isn't an attempt to excuse arrogance and make superiority OK – far from it. This is a call to realise who and what we really are, to get a proper sense of our place in the world.

Our unique self and contribution

Each one of us is made unique. God wanted you and me in the world because we can be someone that nobody else can be. This means that we have a position in the universe that no one else can fill – just through existing.

If we can recognise this, accept who we are as loved by God and his unique creation, made to reflect the divine image in our own personal way, then this will set us free.

We are free to make our own contribution to the world, yes, but also to recognise that our worth doesn't depend on what we can pack into each day but on God's love for us, his own one-off creation.

We are free to rest and to accept the fact that we aren't asked to do everything to save the world, even if we could, to prove that we're OK.

And we are free to sometimes stop and smell the flowers, spend an evening in front of the TV and enjoy a favourite meal, knowing that God made good things for *us* to enjoy – not just everybody else.

I think there's something joyful about seeing someone doing something that they truly enjoy, that really absorbs them and makes them happy, that refreshes and restores them to a balanced sense of well-being. And I can't help thinking that God feels the same way when he sees us taking some time out from trying to carry the world on our shoulders.

God made us out of love and to reflect his glory in the world through our individual combination of gifts, temperament, preferences and talents. He didn't make us to be self-hating slaves.

As the psalmist puts it:

> *I praise you, for I am fearfully and wonderfully made.*
> *Wonderful are your works; that I know very well.*

> *Psalm 139.14 (NRSVA)*

And Genesis:

> *So God created humankind in his image,*
> *in the image of God he created them;*
> *male and female he created them.*

> *Genesis 1.27 (NRSVA)*

Being made in God's image means we need to recognise that there is much in us that comes from God.

This should help us resist the temptation to put ourselves down, call ourselves names, shrug off any talk of our abilities and gifts, to think that we, made in God's image, are somehow defective, worthless or rubbish. That's not humility, as we might be tempted to think, but a self-hatred that does nothing but drag us down.

God's image isn't perfect in any of us but it's still there in every good deed, thought and impulse within us, in every act of beauty and creativity, in every kind smile, and in all our striving to become better people. And there's no great goodness in being so convinced of our unworthiness and lack of ability that we end up just sitting at home doing nothing.

Balance

What we need, as Christians, is balance. We need to find the path between a sense of arrogance and entitlement that says, 'me first and me only' and a crippling dislike of ourselves that convinces us we're never good enough and so should never try.

We need to recognise our faults and limitations while also seeing the good in us. We need to work to improve our understanding of how we can work with our frail, limited, beautiful and loved-by-God selves to love God, our neighbours and ourselves in perfect balance and harmony.

Suggestions for exploration and prayer

- Gather together items (or pictures of items) that represent different aspects of yourself: what you do at church, work or at home, the things you like to learn about, your hobbies and what's important to you as a Christian and human being. Use these to think about who you are, what you can offer and how you might serve God and others.

- Read and meditate on The Parable of the Talents in Matthew 25.14-30 or Luke 19.11-27.

- Are there people or things that make you feel bad about yourself? Could you limit your exposure to them or do something to change the situation?

- Consider whether your life is balanced between work, family, responsibilities, play and time spent with God. If not, are there ways in which you could achieve a better balance?

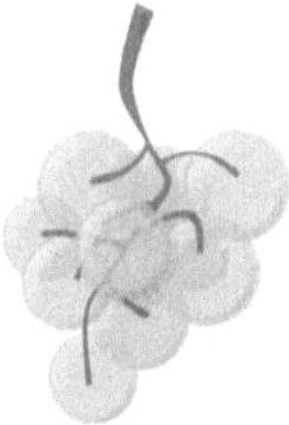

Kindness

What is kindness?

An everyday virtue

Kindness isn't one of those big, important, theological words. It's a rather ordinary, everyday sort of idea.

We tell our children to be kind to one another, we find our day made better by acts of kindness like a stranger holding a door open for us and most of us like to think we're kind, especially to children, animals and people in trouble.

But it's rarely preached about in church or discussed as an important virtue by theologians and philosophers. Yet, there it is, in the middle of the fruit of the Spirit – kindness. Kindness is an attitude of friendliness and generosity, an inclination to be helpful, considerate or humane.

If we spend a lot of time looking at things like Twitter or the news, we can get the impression that there isn't much kindness around in the world. These things like to focus on the bad news because sadly that's what sells. So there seems to be a lot of shouting, division, hatred, prejudice and selfishness. There seem to be a lot of people who are only looking out for themselves and couldn't care less if others get hurt. And there seem to be a lot of people who aren't necessarily out to cause harm – they just don't want to get involved in the problems of others.

Can we see?

But there's a great deal of kindness all around us, if we choose to see it. Kindness can be seen in people who give their own food or clothes to people who are homeless or those who stop what they're doing to help an elderly person struggling with walking or carrying shopping. It can be seen in those who offer their professional services for free or at a low cost to people in need or who hear about a stranger's dream on the Internet and go out of their way to make it come true. Kindness can be seen in those who do something nice for another person just because they can – and without expecting anything back and those who send a card, give a hug or offer a smile to someone who's finding things tough.

Kindness is alive and well in all these people, living ordinary lives in small towns or large cities, in homes large or small, or even in no homes at all. For kindness doesn't depend on having a lot, just on giving what we have. It depends on recognising that we're all in this life together, all human beings, all worthy and loved, suffering, struggling and flawed, and all sometimes in need of a helping hand.

We're all, in our own ways, capable of making this world more beautiful – if we choose. We can all choose to be despairing or cynical about the world, to decide that kindness is for wimps and those who want to be taken advantage of. Or we can choose to believe in goodness, to keep kindness alive, to make another's day a little easier and lighter, trusting that we are following in the footsteps of a God who is both strong and immensely kind.

Can we make a difference?

So, if we want to be kind how can we do it? We can be kind by loving our neighbour.

As we come closer to God and let ourselves be healed and changed by him, we also start to turn outwards towards others, finding it more and more natural to be concerned about them and to want to help them and show them God's kindness.

Then love and service aren't a burden but a joy; kindness

isn't an effort but an expression of our inner selves, and as natural as a flower turning to face the sun. This can be hard when we see so much difficulty and harshness all around us. It can seem like we don't know where to start and we wonder if it will really matter.

But we don't have to change the whole world. We don't have to strain to do what we can't. All we need to do is keep our eyes open to the people we can help in our corner of the world and consider how small kindnesses might brighten their day.

There's a story about a beach covered with thousands of starfish that had been washed up and left stranded by a storm. A girl was walking along picking them up and throwing them back into the sea when someone came up to her and asked why she was bothering as there were far too many for her to save them all. What difference were her efforts making? The girl bent down, picked one up, threw it into the sea and said, 'It made a difference to that one.'

Even if it seems like our small kindnesses are just a tiny moment in an unkind world, we can make a difference somewhere and to someone. And these don't have to be big, dramatic actions.

In the story *The Lion and the Mouse*, Aesop talks about how a mouse comes across a sleeping lion. She's scared and tries to run away but accidentally runs right over the lion's nose. In his anger the lion captures the mouse under his paw in order to kill her but the mouse pleads for her life, promising to repay the lion one day. The lion finds the idea that a mouse could possibly help him ridiculous but lets the mouse go. Soon afterwards the lion is caught in a net. The mouse hears him roaring, runs to help, and saves him by gnawing through the ropes.

The conclusion? No act of kindness, no matter how small, is ever wasted.

Suggestions for exploration and prayer

- If you want ideas about things you can do to be kind *The Little Book of Kindness* by Bernadette Russell (Orion Spring, 2017) has many suggestions for ways to be kind to different people and in various situations.

- Try spending a week looking out for acts of kindness all around you, taking time to notice the positive in daily life.

- Think about people who've been kind to you in the past, or the present. Thank God for them and maybe, if you can, express your appreciation to them as well with a card, a gift or just a thank you.

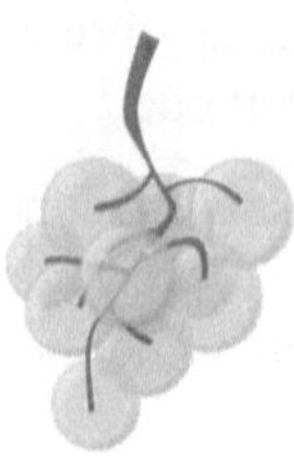

Is God kind?

Images of God

When you try to imagine God, what springs to mind? Perhaps you think of power or judgement, of a supreme being far above us puny humans. Or maybe you think of a saviour, someone who rescues us from sin and death, and on whom we're completely dependent. Maybe in your mind God is a creative genius who set the universe in motion and keeps everything going. God might be a parent – an image that can be positive or negative, depending on your own experiences – or a friend or someone you have an on-off relationship with.

But in all our images and ideas of God, do we find a place for kindness? Does it fit in the character of God at all?

Sometimes we split God up when it comes to kindness. We see God in the Old Testament as harsh, punishing and all about rules, while in the New Testament God is all about love, mercy and kindness. We might even agree with these famous words of Joseph Campbell, an American professor of literature:

> *... it [a computer] seems to me to be an Old Testament god; with a lot of rules and no mercy.*
>
> *Joseph Campbell*

Yet this is a distortion of the truth.

There are some disturbing stories in the Old Testament in which God seems harsh and unkind, and many explanations and ways of understanding why they're there and what they're about, but there are many more examples of God being kind.

Right at the beginning, in Genesis, we see God creating a beautiful and amazing universe and giving us the whole world as a gift to enjoy and cherish – not for his sake but for ours. Then when things go wrong God doesn't give up on us but still cares for humanity, still offers the chance of a relationship, of love, of kind forgiveness and grace.

All through the story of God and Israel we see this over and over – God rescues them from Egypt, leads them through the desert and gives them food, water and a new home. And he does all this no matter how many times they turn away from him, complain, misunderstand and generally get things wrongs.

So the Old Testament isn't all about rules with no mercy.

Also, as Christians we believe that Jesus shows us what God is like. And in Jesus we see someone who talks to a shunned woman at a well (John 4.1–42), heals the sick (Luke 4.38–44), helps out a wedding couple who've run out of wine (John 2.1–12), cries at the death of a friend (John 11.28–37), cares about children (Mark 10:13–16) and refuses to condemn a woman caught in adultery (John 8.1–11).

In Jesus we see someone who is kind, compassionate and caring, and if that is what Jesus is like then that is what God is like. So we can't put a divide between the Old Testament and the New – they both show us the same God, after all.

The image of kindness

We can also know that God is kind because we, who are called to follow God, are led into developing kindness in ourselves. The fruit of the Spirit grows in us as we become more like Christ, the image and reflection of God. And part of that fruit is kindness.

We're capable of kindness as human beings, made in God's image, and that kindness is to be encouraged, nurtured and trained up until it flowers. So our kindness must in some way be a reflection, perhaps very small and pale, of a kind God.

This might be hard to take in. After all, the world is full of rough edges, unkind acts and difficult truths. And sometimes we have ideas and images of God that provide a stern, harsh and even cruel picture, as already mentioned.

Kindness in the world

But the world is also full of kindness. We can see God's kindness to us through the gentle breeze that cools us on a hot day, a cute animal that makes us smile or beautiful flowers growing in the most unlikely places.

We can see kindness through an elderly man caring for his sick wife, a parent giving their child a goodnight kiss or a friend who knows how to make us smile and laugh.

We might also experience the unexpected kindness of strangers who stand up for the bullied, lend a hand, give a smile, let us go ahead of them in a queue, help the homeless and do all these things for people they may never really know – except that they've recognised a sister or brother.

Kindness from heaven

And the world has a God who leaves the place of glory and power to heal, restore, draw close to the rejected and unnoticed, lift heavy burdens, laugh, cry, die for our sins and rise from the dead for us.

God doesn't leave us to stew in our own mistakes and problems. God comes to us in kindness, holds out a helping hand, and is eager to help if we will let him. Not in a 'Look what a mess you've made of things; I suppose I've got to put it all right' sort of way but in a 'Here, I can see things are difficult; will you let me help?' sort of way.

Gods, kings and other important people don't usually lower themselves to such things. But our God does, for our God is kind. So yes, God is kind, despite all our human attempts to make him out to be harsh and judgemental. God is kind and longs for a world in which we reflect his kindness and are all kind to one another.

God is kind, so let us be glad and,

> *As God's chosen ones, holy and beloved, clothe your-selves with compassion, kindness, humility, meekness, and patience.*

> *Colossians 3.12 (NRSVA)*

Suggestions for exploration and prayer

- Look up Bible verses that express God's kindness, and maybe write down any that particularly speak to you.

- Consider and pray about ways in which you might be able to share some of God's kindness with others, however big or small.

- Remember to be kind to yourself as well, by letting go of perfectionism and any feelings that you must always be doing something for others: it's OK to veg out on the sofa sometimes!

Who must we be kind to?

The difficulties of kindness

Let's be honest – some kinds of kindness are easier than others, and we wouldn't be human if we didn't find it easier to be kind to some people than to others. There are people we just don't like, people who seem determined to push us away, and people we feel we don't have time for or who we think aren't our responsibility.

But is this how kindness should work?

The Bible tells us that God is kind even to those who don't deserve it and don't acknowledge it. God is kind to the unkind, the unlovable and the prickly, as well as to those who seem to 'deserve' it. And because God is like this we, who try to love and follow him, need to try to be the same:

> *'But love your enemies, do good, and lend, expecting nothing in return. Your reward will be great, and you will be children of the Most High; for he is kind to the ungrateful and the wicked.'*

> *Luke 6.35 (NRSVA)*

Not that this is an easy thing. It's so much nicer to be kind to our friends, who we know will be kind back some day, or at the least will give us gratitude and praise. It's good to be kind to our friends, of course, but there's more to our calling as disciples than that:

> *'If you love those who love you, what credit is that to you? For even sinners love those who love them. If you do good to those who do good to you, what credit is that to you? For even sinners do the same.'*

> *Luke 6.32-33 (NRSVA)*

We can be kind to colleagues at work, in the hope that they will make our working day easier or develop a good opinion of us that will help us get on well in the office. We might also hope that our boss will notice and give us a good appraisal – or even a pay rise. We can get a glow from helping strangers if it doesn't cost us much and is likely to bring us recognition, or if the cause is a popular one.

I recently heard a talk show host admit that he only put money in the tip jar at his local coffee shop if he was sure that someone would notice. We're sometimes more likely to help if we think someone else will see our good deeds.

This isn't to suggest that kindness is often done from cynical motives but some sorts of kindness come more naturally and, good those these are, we're called to the kindnesses that are harder to show as well.

Kindness without return

We're called to be kind to people who have no way of repaying us – neighbours in countries hit by war, disaster, famine, political upheaval and disease.

We're called to people in our own country, which, although relatively rich and stable, has plenty of people who are unemployed, in need of food banks or sleeping on the streets, or are struggling with loneliness, illness or mental and physical disabilities.

We're called to help strangers who we'll never see again and who will never do us a favour in return, whether or not anyone else is watching. We're called, in fact, to be kind even when it brings us no benefit.

Kindness without judgement

We're called to be kind even to people who we feel don't deserve it – people who we think have brought disaster on their own heads through their lifestyle choices, through bad decisions, through laziness or incompetence or a lack of understanding.

Yet God is kind to such as these, and we are called to be the same. This may mean pointing out (without blame or judgement) the ways in which they're causing themselves problems – it can be kinder in the long run to be honest even if this causes temporary hurt. But it also means giving a second chance where possible, not writing people off, equipping people and walking with them if they'll allow it.

And, after all, who hasn't made a bad decision or two in life or messed up here and there?

I heard a story about a woman who was in a desperate situation. She had lost her job after many difficulties at work, was almost out of money and was about to be thrown out of her flat. She was wandering the streets, cold and hungry, when she came across a café and went in to see if she could work for some food. The woman behind the counter told her this was against company policy but then gave her food and coffee anyway and paid for it herself. She also helped her find a job and she worked her way up to becoming a CEO.

And all this was made possible because at her lowest moment, and despite the fact that many might've blamed her for not holding on to her job, or suggested she wasn't trying hard enough to find a new one, or assumed that she could just get benefits, she was met with kindness.

The stranger who helped had no reason to think she would get anything back for herself or that the woman deserved help – she was just someone who saw a fellow human being in need.

God's kindness is shown supremely in the act of coming to Earth to rescue us from our own disaster of sin, and this shows us the way to go. Some are ungrateful; some won't give us the response we want, and maybe feel we deserve, in return for our kindness.

The trouble is that we can't control people's responses or make them feel how we want them to feel. All we can do is continue with what we believe to be right, not seeking a reward to make ourselves feel better but being content in the knowledge that we're becoming more Christlike and helping to transform our small part of the world into something closer to God's kingdom.

Suggestions for exploration and prayer

- We all have people in our lives we'd rather not have anything to do with. This might be the best option in unsafe situations but otherwise ask God for the grace to find a way to be kinder to them, even if it's just a small smile or a 'how are you?'.

- When tempted to judge people for being in a mess, try to remember that we can all make mistakes and face unexpected disasters. We might find it helpful to remember our own mess-ups and the people who helped us get back on our feet to spur us on to share that kindness with others.

- Try making cards with random acts of kindness written on them and choose one to do each day or week or month, for someone you know or a complete stranger. These might range from opening a door to helping out at a food bank or anything else that you feel able to do.

Generosity

A generous God

How God gives

There's a saying that goes, 'It's better to give than to receive'. I think we can all relate to that. There's a real happiness to be found in looking for the perfect present for someone, wrapping it up and giving to them, and then seeing joy and delight on their face as they open it. And I wonder if you think God feels the same way.

Do you imagine God as generous, as delighting in giving, as someone who gives for the joy of it? Do you think God likes giving us things and seeing us react with happiness? Or do you imagine God as someone who doles out what we need reluctantly or just for his own purposes, and with a stern warning not to waste it?

God's approach to giving can be seen in many different ways.

A generous universe

We can see how God gives in the vastness of our universe, currently thought to have a diameter of 93 billion light years and including millions of galaxies, stars, planets and all sorts of wonders we have yet to discover.

Just our own galaxy has around 250 billion stars. A universe of that size isn't 'necessary', and neither is all the variety and beauty it contains. Yet, the whole of creation exists for the sheer joy and love of it and is given to us to share, explore, enjoy and wonder at.

We see God's generosity in the abundance of life on our planet: an estimated 8.7 million species of plants, animals, birds, reptiles and invertebrates, all different, all adding to the beauty and variety of our planet, and (most at least) bringing joy and delight into our world.

Even the smallest and shortest-lived, even the ones we don't much like, are given their own special place in the world. We take our place in a world which was given to us as a gift to enjoy, care for, understand and explore.

Rowan Williams says,

We exist because of an utterly unconditional generosity. The love God shows in making the world, like the love he shows towards the world once it is created, has no shadow or shred of self-directed purpose in it; it is entirely given for our sake.

Tokens of Trust

A generous relationship

God also shows generosity in his relationship with human beings. Throughout history God has again and again stepped in to help us in our most difficult moments.

He has freed people from slavery, injustice and captivity – in Egypt for the people of Israel and in the end of the slave trade through people like William Wilberforce.

He has brought hope to the hopeless through the message of the gospel and through inspiring people like the Samaritans to give their time to help.

He has provided care and comfort to the unloved, the lonely and the forgotten in those who go out and love as he loves us.

He has freed captives in those who work for prison reform.

He has poured out blessings and given people reasons to celebrate and be happy through births, graduations, marriages, new jobs and second chances.

He has renewed the courage and strength of those who were faltering so that they are ready to listen, encourage and support.

He has brought love into people's lives through the power of his presence and always being ready to hear prayers.

A generous salvation

Then there is God's particular generosity to us in the face of our fallenness and brokenness.

The greatest gift of all, of course, is God himself coming to Earth, choosing freely to live with us, suffer, die and rise again for us, to set us free from our sin out of a generous desire to put things right for us. Jesus is God's gift of love to the world, a gift that couldn't be greater, a gift freely given, a wild and impossible declaration of generosity and love.

And Jesus also shows us what God's generosity is like when he turns water into gallons of good wine (John 2.1–12), feeds 5,000 people and still has basketfuls of leftovers (Matthew 14.13–21) and fills fishing nets to breaking point (Luke 5.1–11).

The generosity here is extravagant, even wasteful we might think, going far beyond carefully giving us just what we need.

There was no need at the wedding in Cana to give already drunk people so much good wine but Jesus gave it in joyful generosity – a sign that joyful giving and celebration are signs of God's kingdom.

There was no need for so many leftovers when feeding the

hungry crowds who'd followed Jesus out into the country-side but this miracle turned the chore of feeding people into a feast to which anyone who wanted could come.

There was no need for quite so many fish when the fishermen's nets were empty but again God's presence brought abundance and celebration to an everyday need, not just making it possible to pay the bills but adding more to gladden hearts.

Generosity is shown in God opening his arms, running to us like the father in the story of the prodigal son (Luke 15: 11–32), and inviting us to be his children, to be close to him and know ourselves loved by him.

A generous response

So, we are children of a generous God, living in a world that, for all its flaws and darkness, reflects something of his desire for us to have good things and be joyful.

Generosity is part of God's very nature, and so as his children, growing ever more like him, generosity needs to expand and grow and flow out of us also. We need to really experience, take in and enjoy God's generosity so that it can flow into our lives and then outwards to others.

Then we can experience the joy not only of receiving but also of giving, not only of seeing and understanding what God has given us and promises to give us in the future but also of making the experience of generosity a reality in the lives of others.

Suggestions for exploration and prayer

- Maybe go out into nature or look up at the night sky and reflect on the abundant beauty of our world and the universe, giving thanks for the good things all around us. You could also think about places you have been in the world and the good things there.

- **Reflect on a** Bible verse about God's goodness and generosity. As you do, drink some water to remind you of Jesus' promise of living water to restore us. You could also write a prayer of thanksgiving on a piece of paper or cardboard cut into a droplet shape.

- Try writing down all the ways in which God has shown to you, personally, goodness and generosity. You could also draw things to represent them or use a mind map or find any other way of doing it that appeals to you.

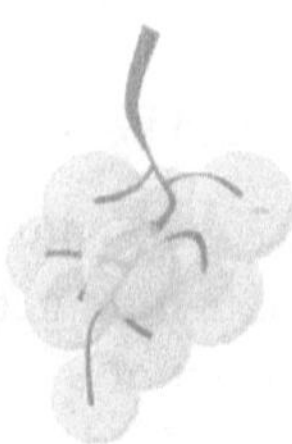

Generous people

The Diocese of Ely in the Church of England uses the following as its vision statement:

We pray to be generous and visible people of Jesus Christ.

This sounds inspiring but what does it mean to be generous people?

Money

The first thing that might spring to mind is giving money to the Church and other good causes. And you might be groaning a bit at the idea of being told to give more – we can all get a bit defensive about our money sometimes. But our use of money, our attitude to it, and what we will or won't do to get it and hold on to it, are all very important.

The Bible has much to say about the use and misuse of money.

It warns us of the dangers of getting so attached to it that we forget what really matters and grasp it selfishly to ourselves, always wanting more and doing anything to get it, while others struggle and suffer. Not for nothing does the Bible say,

For the love of money is a root of all kinds of evil, and in their eagerness to be rich some have wandered away from the faith and pierced themselves with many pains.

1 Timothy 6.10 (NRSVA)

Jesus even tells us that we have to choose: do we serve God or money?

For some, attachment to money may come from a background of poverty and a fear of slipping back into that. In contrast, for others it may come from a sense of entitlement because they've always had money and never needed to worry about it. But whatever the reason for holding on tight we need to remember that, while money makes a lot of things easier, it can't buy us family or friends or stop us getting ill.

Neither is it necessary to enjoy many of the things that make us smile or laugh or enjoy being alive. So it's important to think about whether we're holding on too tightly to money and if opening our hands a little and being generous where we can might in fact be good for both others and ourselves.

Yet there is more to generosity than thinking we really should be giving more money to good causes. Generosity applies in all areas of life and there are many opportunities to be generous even if we don't have much money to spend.

Time

We can be generous with our time, listening to someone who's ill, scared or lonely. We can help someone learn a new skill or listen to their ideas and dreams and plans. We can mend, cook, clean, shop or garden for someone who's unable to do it themselves because of illness or old age or just having too much on.

Alternatively, we can take time to rejoice and be glad for someone who wants to celebrate passing an exam, getting their driving licence, getting out of hospital or finishing a big project.

It's not just the people who are struggling who need our time but also people who are glad and want someone to share it with. In a world that keeps moving faster, offering someone a bit of time can be a beautiful gift.

This is especially true for those people who feel left behind as others rush about keeping manically busy – these might be people who are unemployed, housebound, retired, chronically ill or at home with small children.

Many of us feel like we don't have any time – and it's true that life is busy and we all need some moments on the sofa doing nothing. But perhaps there are a few slots here and there that we could offer to others.

Talents and skills

We can also be generous with our abilities. We can do this by making an effort to notice what would make other people's lives better and offering our help.

Sometimes it can seem like this is only for the more outgoing and super-talented people but that isn't true. Everyone can make a contribution, whether it's making beautiful things, cooking a nice meal or volunteering to help out with anything from washing up to administration to directing a major event.

Whatever we have to offer it can do real and lasting good. All these things and more are opportunities for us to be generous with the things we can do. They are chances to offer our passions and skills in the service of others. For we're given them not just for ourselves or to enable us to make money but also for the sake of others, so that we can all help to make the world a brighter and more generous place.

Attitudes

Another way of being generous has to do with how we think about people.

When a person rushes past us without saying hello we can assume they're rude and spend our time brooding and getting offended or wondering what we've done wrong.

When someone snaps or treads on our toes (literally or metaphorically) we can assume they've done it on purpose because they're a bad person or they don't like us.

Or, we can take a more generous approach and think maybe they're tired, worried or have a lot on their minds. We can think that perhaps they didn't mean to or don't understand what they've done wrong or consider that maybe their behaviour comes from pain or trouble of their own.

This is a generosity of mind and spirit that's not quick to take offence and write off the other person or to assume we've done something wrong but is willing to think the best of others and not see malice where it might not exist.

We can apply the same logic in many situations where our first reaction to someone else's behaviour might be to think the worst of them without stopping to consider what else could be going on.

There are many ways to be generous people of Jesus Christ and, as the fruit of the Spirit grows in us and we gradually reflect more and more of God's nature, our own generosity will unfold into a beautiful blessing for those around us.

Suggestions for exploration and prayer

- To explore ways in which you could be more generous with your money, time, skills or attitudes you could cut out a flower (or flowers) and on each petal write an idea for what you could do in each area. Put it somewhere you'll see it and be reminded to try to be more generous.

- Try making a model of something that you could share with others in the week or weeks ahead, maybe out of plasticine or clay or something like Lego bricks.

- When you're tempted to think the worst of a person's actions or motivations think about or write down what other, more positive, explanations there might be for what they do or say.

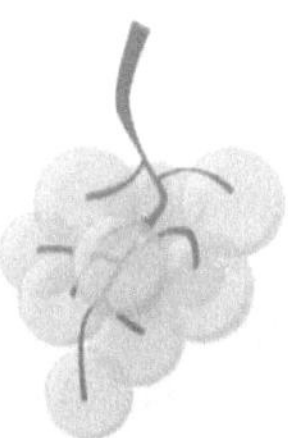

Gratitude and generosity

Becoming more generous

How can we become more generous people?

Well we could grit our teeth and make ourselves do it but on the other hand the Bible tells us that,

> *Each of you must give as you have made up your mind, not reluctantly or under compulsion, for God loves a cheerful giver.*

> *2 Corinthians 9.7 (NRSVA)*

So perhaps forced generosity is not the way to go. And while we do sometimes have to do things we really don't want to do, I don't think in this case it would work very well. Instead we might find ourselves doing the minimum or giving the minimum we can get away with, and possibly being quite grumpy about it in a way that puts other people off.

Another, perhaps gentler, way to become more generous is to first become more grateful for what we have. This sounds contradictory because gratitude is about what we get, while generosity is about what we give, but studies have shown that having a more grateful attitude and acknowledging what you've got makes you more likely to be generous to others.

The benefits of gratitude

John Kralik, in his book *A Simple Act of Gratitude*, talks about a time when he was 53 and everything was going wrong. His business was failing, he was getting divorced for the second time, family relationships were strained, and he was living in a rundown uncomfortable apartment in Los Angeles. But one New Year's Day, in the middle of all this, he decided to write one thank you note a day for a year in order to make himself find something to be grateful for every day. And this helped him shift his focus towards the positive and become more outward-looking, enhancing his life in many ways, even though he continued to face many difficulties.

When we're grateful, we recognise the good things in our lives and are freed from some of our worries and fears, helping us to be more outward-looking rather than preoccupied with ourselves. We become happier, more satisfied and less materialistic, making it easier for us to share what we have without fretting that we might lose out.

This also guards us against the temptation to give in order to get something back – which is a step towards manipulating people for our own ends rather than a step towards true generosity. And as we see what we've been given, we hopefully spend less time focusing in on our own problems and become more joyful and inclined to share that joy with others.

Our hands can open when we're less anxious and negative, and we are set free to give as we have received, not out of some kind of grudging sense of duty but because we want to spread happiness.

What do we look at?

We all have difficult times in our lives – times when life is hard, dark and even heartbreaking; periods when we feel we have nothing left and nothing to give. We may have times when we feel we've lost everything – and it's right to be honest about that and not place unrealistic expectations on ourselves and others at times of great loss and hurt.

But we can also train ourselves to look for the bright spots in everyday life, the small things that keep us going.

Do we have a home, food, water, family or a friend? We tend to take these for granted but not everyone has all or even any of these things and so they are things to be grateful for.

Has someone done us a favour, told a joke that made us smile or groan, given us another chance to get something right? Then we can remember such things with gratitude.

Have we seen a glimpse of nature, stroked a pet, enjoyed some music, had a good cup of coffee or encountered a beautiful building or piece of art? These too are gifts.

Can we remember with gratitude the ways in which God has stood by us, never letting us fall beyond hope and carrying us through difficulties?

And are we aware of the ways in which our faith has been supported and encouraged by fellow Christians, both those we know and ones far away or who lived a long time before us? These are gifts to us as well.

There's a lot of pressure on us to look at what's negative in the world, mostly coming from the news and social media, but it can do us a lot of good to look out for the good things as well. And as we look for the good things, and start to develop a habit of recognising and celebrating them, we also need to remember to pass that goodness on.

We need to make generosity a contagious thing that spreads from God to us and outwards to other people. We need to notice when we can be generous and take advantage of the opportunities, however big or small they may be, to share goodness and joy.

It's important to resist the pressure to see only darkness. It's important not to let cynicism and despair overtake us or to let difficulties overwhelm us.

We need to exercise our power to choose how we react to the world, to choose whether we see darkness everywhere or the points of light that are the good things in the world. And we need to let ourselves be points of light as well, opening our hearts, hands, minds and wallets to pass on to others the generosity God has shown to us. And we do this because we're children of a God who delights to give generously and calls on us to share in that delight and goodness.

Suggestions for exploration and prayer

- You could take a leaf out of John Kralik's book and write a thank you note every day for a while. These could be to other people or you could write thank you notes to God as a basis for prayer.

- A similar idea is to write down just a line each day about something that has happened during the day which you are grateful for and take them out and read them when tempted to think everything is dark.

- Are there ways in which you feel you could be more generous – with time, money or skills? Try investigating what you might be able to give or do gladly and openly.

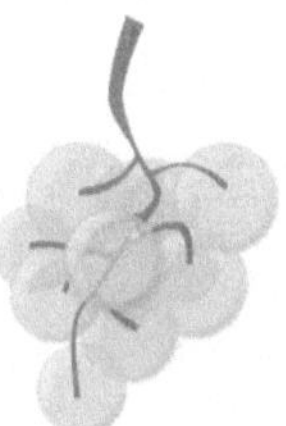

JOY, PEACE AND SELF-CONTROL

In this second part of the book I consider joy, peace and self-control.

These three aspects of the fruit of the Spirit focus on our internal state, on how we are inside. They have external elements as well, because if we are joyful, peaceful and self-controlled this can only have positive influences on others, but they start inside us.

Joy is a sign of God's kingdom:

For the kingdom of God is ... righteousness and peace and joy in the Holy Spirit.

Romans 14.17 (NRSVA)

Jesus promises us that peace is our inheritance when he says,

Peace I leave with you; my peace I give to you. I do not give to you as the world gives. Do not let your hearts be troubled, and do not let them be afraid.

John 14.27 (NRSVA)

And self-control, although it can seem a negative thing if we think of it as meaning we can't do what we want, leads us to greater rewards and a longer-lasting happiness.

Athletes exercise self-control in all things; they do it to receive a perishable garland, but we an imperishable one.

1 Corinthians 9.25 (NRSVA)

Joy

Joy and happiness

Joy versus happiness?

Are joy and happiness the same thing?

There's a tendency these days to say no and to say that happiness is a shallow thing, dependent on circumstances and brief pleasures like eating an ice cream or the smell of a new car, while joy is a gift from God that lasts for ever. Happiness, people claim, is an emotion while joy isn't.

It's further claimed that happiness is a worldly thing chased after by people who don't know God and who are unable to get real joy.

Thus,

> *... there is a secret belief amongst some men that God is displeased with man's happiness; and in consequence they slink about creation, ashamed and afraid to enjoy themselves.*
>
> *Arthur Helps, Companions of My Solitude*

Yet, the idea that joy and happiness are different would be alien to most Christians throughout history.

C.S. Lewis picks up on this idea in *The Screwtape Letters*. In this series of letters from a senior to a junior devil there comes a point when the junior devil lets someone he's trying to tempt away from God enjoy some simple pleasures for their own sake, and the senior devil isn't pleased:

> *And now for your blunders. On your own showing you first of all allowed the patient to read a book he really enjoyed, because he enjoyed it and not in order to make clever remarks about it to his new friends. In the second*

place, you allowed him to walk down to the old mill and have tea there – a walk through country he really likes, and taken alone. In other words you allowed him two real positive Pleasures. Were you so ignorant as not to see the danger of this?

C.S. Lewis, The Screwtape Letters

Lewis's point is that simple happiness brings us in touch with reality, with God, and doing things that make us happy is thus a source of joy that brings us closer to God. Happiness, pleasure and joy are here intertwined. Trying to force apart two words that are clearly so similar in meaning is a very modern idea and one not really supported by the Bible.

John Piper writes that,

If you have nice little categories for 'joy is what Christians have' and 'happiness is what the world has,' you can scrap those when you go to the Bible, because the Bible is indiscriminate in its uses of the language of happiness and joy and contentment and satisfaction.

John Piper, Let Your Passion Be Single

Both joy and happiness are pleasurable emotions, and both are found in Bible passages that speak of joy and happiness as being the same thing.

Take, for example:

Then shall the young women rejoice in the dance,
and the young men and the old shall be merry.
I will turn their mourning into joy,
I will comfort them, and give them gladness for sorrow.

Jeremiah 31.13 (NRSVA)

Here, joy is equated with merriness and gladness – both of which are synonyms for happiness. And we can't be joyful but sad. There's no such thing as a miserable, joyful person. To be joyful means to be happy. Christians should be growing in joy and growing in happiness.

We can't force the emotion of happiness out of joy or the emotion of joy out of happiness.

True versus false

Of course, there are forms of pleasure which are harmful. There are things which seem to be about happiness but are really distortions of it, twisting it away from its true nature to meet another end like power or self-gratification without concern for others.

Happiness in the sufferings of others is clearly not a joyful thing but an attempt to feel more powerful or to get revenge. Happiness can be distorted and misused in ways that do nothing but harm and take us far away from what happiness and joy are really meant to be.

And there's a happiness that leaves us unsatisfied not because it's harmful but because it doesn't go deep enough to truly satisfy our desire for joy. The latest thrill or fad, a new possession or relationship, can give us a burst of happiness, but as we all know the gloss wears off after a while and what seemed so new and exciting becomes ordinary and normal.

Then we can fall into the trap of constantly chasing after the next thing we think will make us happy without realising that we're stuck in a cycle of always thinking that newer is better. And in doing this we miss out on the deeper happiness that's available to us if we're able to look deeper and resist giving up on things as soon as the first excitement is gone.

Happiness can be either temporary or permanent in our lives but we don't need to try to split happiness and joy from each other to cope with this.

Finding happiness

We just need to concentrate on what makes us truly happy in the long term and beware of putting all our hope in fleeting pleasures.

We can find happiness in things like tending a garden and seeing it grow and change through the seasons or spending time on other creative things – finding joy in being the creative beings God formed us to be and bringing beauty into the world.

We can join a choir or an orchestra or make music at home if that makes us happy. Music lifts us up out of ourselves and can be used to praise God as well.

Exercise also makes us happy while keeping us in good health, and if we can combine it with being outside then the benefits are even greater. This way we take care of the bodies and minds God gave us and find another source of happiness.

And we can find happiness by trying to help others find theirs.

There was once a seminar in which the speaker asked all the people attending to write their name on a balloon. Then the balloons were taken away into another room and the attendees were let in and told to find their own name. There was chaos as everyone pushed past each other to find their own balloon, colliding with each other and falling over their feet. After five minutes no one had found their balloon. They were then asked to pick up a random balloon and give it to the person whose name was written on it. Within a few minutes everyone had their own balloon.

The speaker said: 'This is what happens in life. We all look frantically for our own happiness, not knowing where to find it. Yet if we all look for other people's happiness then we find our own.'

It's not that there's anything wrong with the small pleasures of life, like a cup of coffee or new clothes, but we need a sense of proportion about what really matters and where to find true happiness and joy.

Joy and happiness go hand in hand, and we only need to discover where real, true and lasting joy and happiness are to be found.

Suggestions for exploration and prayer

- Bubble prayers can be a fun way to pray and bring a little happiness into your prayer times. Get hold of a bubble blowing tub and with each bubble you blow think of something that fills you with joy and happiness and thank God for it.

- You could try writing a psalm or song of praise and joy: either just for you and God or to share with others.

- Consider what makes you happy: if they are good things, then can you do more of them? If they are perhaps less good could you replace them with something else?

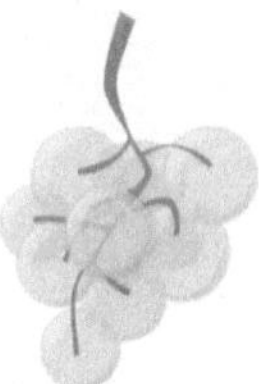

The two thieves

In *The Wisdom House,* Rob Parsons tells us that there are two things which will steal our joy. One of these is hankering after the past and the other is looking too much to the future.

The past

Many of us have done it – looked back to our youth and said things were much better then. Summers were hotter and longer and there was snow every winter. People had better manners and everyone knew their neighbours. There was less pressure on everyone. Young people behaved so much better, and so on.

The thing is that we sometimes edit out the bad bits, and every generation thinks the world is on a downward path. Even in the 8th century BC the Greek poet Hesiod said:

> *I see no hope for the future of our people if they are dependent on frivolous youth of today, for certainly all youth are reckless beyond words... When I was young, we were taught to be discreet and respectful of elders, but the present youth are exceedingly wise [disrespectful] and impatient of restraint.*

We can laugh at this but there's also a danger of letting nostalgia steal our joy as we sigh after the perfect days of our partly imagined past. Of course, as we grow older we do meet new pressures and difficulties but we may also forget the hard parts we've already been through.

As children and teenagers, we chafe under the restraints imposed by parents and school, wishing we could be grown-up and able to make our own choices. We worry about fitting in, whether we're 'normal', and romantic and social rejections feel like major disasters. We're pressured by exams, the need to choose a career, find a partner. We might have to deal with a family break-up or encounter death for the first time.

The past isn't really the golden era we can sometimes see it as, and jealously wishing ourselves back in a time that's gone, instead of being thankful for what was good and acknowledging what was bad, will only make us sad and bitter.

The future

Then there's looking too much into the future.

Dreams about the future are popular and people come up with all sorts of ideas about both how their own lives will turn out and the future of humanity as a whole.

If you've ever seen the cartoon *The Jetsons* you'll have seen a version of the future in which families are still the 1950s ideal of father going out to work, mother at home, two children and a dog. Yet people live in towers in the sky, everything is automatic and done by robots, and the working day is only four hours.

Some visions of the future are positive and others are more anxiety-laden; some are realistic and some look rather dated now but they all have one thing in common – they aren't real.

Planning is good and helpful, as is hope that encourages us to get up and work towards our goals and dreams. We sometimes need to think ahead to solve our problems, increase our chances of success, or to try to solve some of the world's problems. Without these things we may drift along with no real growth or progress but filled with a sense of pointlessness.

But all too often we think that we'll only be happy when

some future event happens. This might be winning the lottery, losing weight, getting a better job, getting married, the kids growing up and being less dependent on us, retiring – the list goes on endlessly. Whatever it is we pin our hopes on, we push our happiness and joy into the future and some imagined circumstances still to come.

In these ways both the future and the past can steal our joy if we let them – but we don't have to let them. We can be thankful for the good things of the past and the grace that got us through the difficulties, and we can hope, work and plan for the future without pinning all our joy and happiness on it.

The present

For the only time we really have in which to experience joy is now. We can't recapture past glories or undo past mistakes. And we can't depend on some future turn of events that may not happen or which may be different from how we expected. Yet we often pass through the present not really noticing it because we're stuck in the past or the future.

When we're at work we long to be on holiday – yet when we're on holiday we worry about what's piling up on our desks for us to do when we return.

And as we live in the future, we miss opportunities to appreciate a sunny day, a friendly colleague, the satisfaction of doing a good job: all the small daily uplifting moments.

And we can go the other way, worrying about whether we should've made different decisions yesterday, last week, last month or even longer ago, even though we can't change them now.

In doing this we miss present opportunities to make decisions and take actions that'll bring us joy right now, like saying yes to an offer of a coffee, spending time with family or friends, spending time with God and feeling the joy he offers us.

Now is the time in which to grasp joy and let it fill us. Now is full of opportunities in which to find joy if we can focus on it and avoid looking too much to the future or too much to the past.

For we find,

> *Happiness… not in another place but this place,*
> *not for another hour but this hour.*
>
> Walt Whitman, *A Song for Occupations*

Suggestions for exploration and prayer

- Try reading Rob Parsons' book *The Wisdom House: Because You Don't Always Have To Learn The Hard Way* (Hodder & Stoughton, 2014).

- Mindfulness is a good way to train yourself to focus on the present instead of the past or future.

- Try to be aware of what is happening right now in your life, and consider where you might see God at work in it. Consider keeping a journal or scrapbook to remind you of what has happened each day and the good moments in life.

Joy and wholeness

Facing our emotions

When we've struggled for a while in life we can forget what joy and happiness are like. The days merge into one another and we get used to being flat, sad or worried.

We might muddle along saying we're fine, to ourselves and others, and pushing away any hint of sadness, anxiety, frustration or depression with food or alcohol or binge-watching TV, or anything else that deadens our feelings for a while.

But the trouble is that you can't choose which emotions to have and which to ignore.

When in emotional pain we can choose one of three ways to deal with it.

1 We can fix whatever went wrong, if possible.
2 We can express our pain if we can't fix the problem.
3 Or we can deny and suppress our 'negative' emotions.

The first two are helpful and healing but the third can end up making things worse. This is because pushing away the 'bad' emotions also removes the 'good' ones and leaves us numb – it's just how it works. And when we become numb we can slip into depression or despair. We can also end up taking out our buried emotions in inappropriate ways.

It's like the classic story of the person who gets angry with his boss but can't express that anger, so goes home and shouts at his wife, who shouts at the children, who kick the cat.

So, if we want to be better at experiencing joy we need the courage to face all our emotions – including the anger we don't want to admit to, the anxiety that keeps us up at night and the jealousy that burns in us when we see other people doing better than we are.

The only real and lasting way to release the hold of these emotions is to work through them, experience them, resolve their causes, learn what they're trying to tell us, and come to peace with the whole range of feelings that make up a human being. It's then that we grow in wholeness, get some healing, and increase our capacity to experience positive feelings, like love, peace and joy. Because as we acknowledge the negative feelings so too the positive ones can come out and be acknowledged, and as we heal we start to find new wonder and delight where before we might have thought a bland, dull existence was all that we could hope for.

Real joy

And when that joy starts to grow it will be real joy. It will be a joy that knows all about difficulties, pains and disappointments but sings anyway because it also knows about the beauty of sunsets, the comfort of being with people who love you, the triumph of not letting yourself be controlled by hurts and negativity, the blessing of being loved by God.

Joy doesn't ignore reality but it understands that there's a greater reality that gives us hope and strength, for

> *Joy is not the absence of pain. Joy is the awareness of God's loving presence within you.*

> *John Catoir*

Joy knows that light will always ultimately chase away darkness, even if darkness seems to win for a while. It knows that good will always ultimately defeat evil, even if all we can currently see is trouble and chaos. It knows that God remains at our side even when everyone else deserts us, even if we don't always remember this.

It's the kind of attitude shown in the story about a woman who was lying ill in bed for months and yet delighted in and thanked God for a bird that sang outside her window every morning. She didn't forget her pain and suffering, or pretend it didn't exist, but she did manage to find a source of joy even within these difficult circumstances.

Growing joy

Of course, we can't just snap our fingers and be joyful. Growing fruit is a long process that takes work and patience, the right environment and weather conditions, and a determination to keep working on it. We need to remember that,

> *Joy is the experience of knowing that you are unconditionally loved and that nothing – sickness, failure, emotional distress, oppression, war, or even death – can take that love away... Joy does not simply happen to us. We have to choose joy and keep choosing it every day. It is a choice based on the knowledge that we belong to God and have found in God our refuge and our safety, and that nothing, not even death, can take God away from us.*

> *Henri Nouwen*

So we must keep choosing to look for joy, despite all the forces pulling us away from it, despite the problems we face and see around us.

We need to decide to try to sink our roots deeper into God each day.

We need to decide to focus on good things instead of just bad ones.

We need to decide to try to remember what we have to be grateful for.

We need to surround ourselves with things that are beautiful or funny or comforting.

Philippians tells us:

> *Finally, beloved, whatever is true, whatever is honoura-*
> *ble, whatever is just, whatever is pure, whatever is pleas-*
> *ing, whatever is commendable, if there is any excellence*
> *and if there is anything worthy of praise, think about these*
> *things.*
>
> *Philippians 4.8 (NRSVA)*

And there is a Jewish saying which goes,

> *At the judgement day a man will be called to account for*
> *all the good things he might have enjoyed and did not*
> *enjoy.*

For it is in thinking about the things that are good, and enjoying the things that are good, that we begin to see God at work around us and recognise that there is a place for joy in our lives.

Suggestions for exploration and prayer

- Try making a paper chain. On each piece of the chain write something that is good in your life or the world, that you're grateful for or that you want to celebrate.

- Pet prayer rocks can be used to remind you to pray, and they might make you smile at the same time! Find a rock, stick on some googly eyes and some hair (maybe made out of wool), and leave it somewhere you'll notice it and remember to think about good things that you want to praise God for.

- Decorate a jar in a way you like and then write joyful things on lollipop sticks and put them in the jar. When you feel you need some more joy and happiness in your life you can pick them out and read them.

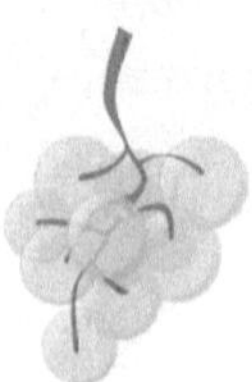

Peace

What is peace?

The Hiroshima Peace Memorial Atomic Bomb Dome stands on the site of the first atomic bomb attack in history – on the 6th August 1945. Outside it there's a banner reading 'Peace'.

Just one simple word, yet it sums up so much grief about the past and hope for the future.

So many of us long for peace, yet we hear so much about war and violence and uncertainty. We may spend our days worrying about our families, our jobs, the bills, our health, the environment… The list goes on.

Yet God promises us peace, and peace is a sign of the Spirit at work within us. When the Bible speaks of peace it is often talking about either the Hebrew concept of *shalom* or the Greek idea of *ēirenē*.

Shalom

If you were to throw a thousand threads onto a table they wouldn't make a fabric. They would just be a pile of threads. They become a fabric when the threads are woven together, under and over and through each other. The more they depend on each other the more beautiful they become. And the more they're tied together the stronger and warmer they are.

And *shalom* is like this.

The word *shalom* refers to a concept, a dream and a promise.

It's a promise of wholeness, health, completeness and peace for ourselves and for the whole world.

It's a promise that injustice will end and the rich will no longer exploit the poor.

The broken and sad will be healed and comforted.

Countries won't go to war against each other and no one will leave in fear of violence.

The Earth itself will no longer be torn apart, or experience violence, damage or decay.

It's never just about an absence of war or trouble but about everything that makes for our highest good. It's about friendship, contentment, security and health. It's about abundance, tranquillity and harmony for all people and the natural world.

We still wait for that *shalom* to come fully, for it comes with the full establishing of God's kingdom on Earth.

Yet there are signs already, shoots coming up in the darkness and the cold, like flowers that appear in winter.

Wherever injustice is challenged and set right.

Where rich people use their wealth to help the poor.

Where someone draws alongside a suffering person to help or just stand with them.

Where peacemakers go bravely into difficult situations and people defend others from violence.

Where people work to protect and preserve God's creation.

Where we depend on each other, work together for good, cooperate and draw together; where we search for unity, goodness and the good of all, there the beautiful fabric of *shalom* appears.

There we can already see God's *shalom* appearing on Earth.

Eirēnē

Imagine you see someone standing on the shore of an island while a huge storm blows massive waves over the sea walls and the wind howls furiously. Imagine this person is standing with his hands in his pockets and looking completely calm. Imagine he's able to look, act and feel calm despite the chaos all around him.

This is what *eirēnē* is like.

It's an inner peace and tranquillity, contentment and serenity regardless of circumstances – because we have confidence in something higher than circumstances.

Henri Nouwen tells of his experience of meeting a disabled person called Adam. Adam could do almost nothing for himself and needed constant help. He was someone we might look on with pity and think of as a person to care for without any way of giving something back.

Yet upon spending time with him Nouwen found that Adam, in his vulnerability and dependence, was full of an inner peace that affected him deeply. Adam had no way out of his situation, could do nothing to help himself, and yet this didn't stop him receiving God's gift of inner peace.

Eirēnē is a peace that can't be destroyed by the situations we face although, being human, we may vary in how much we're able to hold on to our awareness of it.

For,

> *Peace and love are always alive in us, but we are not always alive to love and peace.*
>
> *Julian of Norwich, Revelations of Divine Love*

Eirēnē is also about joining together things that have been separated or disturbed, giving us a sense of setting things right, bringing us and God together and at one in peace and harmony.

God offers us this peace in Jesus, who sets things right between us and God, ending the division caused by sin and restoring us to how we were meant to be:

> *For in him all the fullness of God was pleased to dwell, and through him God was pleased to reconcile to himself all things, whether on earth or in heaven, by making peace through the blood of his cross.*

> *Colossians 1.19-20 (NRSVA)*

And this sense of bringing together in peace and harmony also extends to our relationships with each other, for *shalom* and *eirēnē* overlap with each other.

Both not either

And so, of course, we need both.

People at war with themselves and others, full of anger and hatred, can't be part of any move towards peace. And we can't reach any kind of real peace without recognising our need for each other and the importance of justice, righteousness, freedom and care for us and our planet. So, we need to let God give us that inner peace, that *eirēnē*. We need openness and a recognition of our need for peace within ourselves because both peace and war spring from what's within us. And we need to find ways to work for wider peace and goodness outside ourselves as well.

Then we can see the signs of *shalom* growing around us, get ready for God's kingdom of peace, and play our part in working for the peace that will last for ever.

Suggestions for exploration and prayer

- When watching the news or reading a newspaper and hearing about conflict and trouble try to imagine what life might be like for the people caught up in those events and hold them before God in prayer. You might find it helpful to make a paper dove (you can find instructions on the Internet) and write a name or word that reminds you to pray for that place and people.

- Look at pictures of different types of shoes from around the world. Imagine what your life might be like if you were a person who wore worn-out sandals or boots with holes in or had no shoes at all. Every time you put your shoes on pray for those who live in difficult or dangerous circumstances.

- Consider the things in your life that might be stopping you experiencing God's peace within yourself. Write these down (or draw pictures to represent them or use any other way to express them that appeals to you) and offer them to God, asking for greater peace in your life.

Inner peace

Picture of peace

There's a story about a man who was looking for the perfect picture of peace. He looked everywhere but couldn't find one he was happy with so he announced a contest to produce one instead. Artists from all over the world worked hard and sent in their creations, until the great day arrived when the perfect painting would be chosen.

The judges unveiled one after another while a crowd watched in anticipation until only two pictures were left. As the judges removed the cover from one of them a hush fell over the audience. The picture showed a smooth lake with trees reflected in its waters, sheep grazing quietly along the shore. Everyone sighed contentedly at the image and imagined themselves there, resting on the lake's bank. Surely this was the winning entry?

But then the last picture was revealed and the crowd gasped with surprise. This picture showed a huge waterfall crashing down from a great height on to jagged rocks. There were dark, threatening storm clouds looming overhead. And there was one solitary small tree clinging desperately to the rocks at the bottom of the waterfall.

This surely didn't show peace? What was the artist thinking? Yet in the tree there was a little bird in a nest, calmly sitting on her eggs, apparently undisturbed by the crashing and chaos all around her. And in her quiet sitting she radiated the kind of peace that transcends all troubles, worries and difficulties.

The work of inner peace

I've already mentioned inner peace a couple of times. To be honest I wouldn't blame you if you were thinking that this is all very well but inner peace isn't all that easy to come by. If you're thinking that, well yes, you're right.

When you're trying to juggle a job, family, money worries and ill relatives, on top of being bombarded with world news, social media making you think everyone is having a better time than you, and wondering if you really know what you're doing, inner peace can seem like a distant dream. Yet inner peace can be found even if everything is crashing about around you.

For this peace isn't a product of our circumstances; it doesn't depend on whether we've been having a good day, week, month or year. You don't have to be a super spiritual monk or nun praying and meditating all day either. Instead inner peace can be achieved by all of us, everywhere and in all the changing circumstances of our lives.

But it's not just a case of wanting inner peace and it just arriving neatly packaged. There's both good and bad news here.

The bad news

The bad news is that inner peace does take work and time. It asks us to lay aside all the things that crowd in and demand our attention in order to sit quietly with God and let him refresh us. It's not a quick fix, take two tablets three times a day, kind of thing.

Instead it's more like training for a marathon if up to now you've been a couch potato. We can't just jump up from EastEnders one day and go out to run 26.2 miles. Instead we must start by running for a minute or two, then build that up over weeks and months, throw in some strength training, get advice on nutrition, and above all stick to a training regime regardless of wind, rain or blazing sun, the kind of day we've had and whether or not we feel like it.

And the same is true if we want to grow the fruit of peace within us. We must take time each day to be with God in prayer, contemplation and study of Scripture, building this up over time and with experience. We need to learn from the people who've passed this way before us and left us the benefit of their wisdom and experience, whether it's through reading, courses, podcasts, blogs, sermons or talking to another Christian we trust.

We need to ask for inner peace, accept it and strengthen it within us every day through faith and dependence on God, so that all those many things bombarding us can't destroy our inner peace, even if they shake it around a bit. We need to be a bit more like the bird in the story, and cultivate our own peace that outside circumstances can't shake.

The good news

The good news is that God knows how hard it is and doesn't leave us to it, waiting impatiently at a finish line for us to hurry up and finish the marathon. God is alongside us all the way, and even before we take our first step. God is our training partner, chief cheerleader and motivator.

When we want to pray but are stuck the Spirit helps us:

> *Likewise the Spirit helps us in our weakness; for we do not know how to pray as we ought, but that very Spirit intercedes with sighs too deep for words.*
>
> *Romans 8.26 (NRSVA)*

It's not that the Spirit demands peace from us and leaves it to us to produce it. Instead peace is a gift to us to be grown, nurtured and encouraged with the help and encouragement of God and our fellow Christians. So, long and hard though the path may be, there is good news – God has given us peace, shown us how to grow it and sticks around to help us.

God knows about the storm clouds and the surging waters and helps us find a way to nurture peace within them.

Suggestions for exploration and prayer

- When our hearts and minds are troubled it can be hard to come up with our own prayers. Try using some pre-written prayers from a service book or anthology when you don't know what to say. These contain many treasures and can help us see that we're not alone in feeling how we do. One example is *The Book of a Thousand Prayers*, compiled by Angela Ashwin (Zondervan, 2002).

- Calming music such as Taizé chants or Celtic hymns and songs can soothe us and lead us to a greater awareness of God's presence.

- Take some time each day, even if you can only manage a minute or two, to stop, breathe, remember God is with you and say a few words of prayer.

- Look for a prayer for peace, maybe the *Collect for Peace* from the Church of England; write it down and put it up somewhere you can see and remember it.

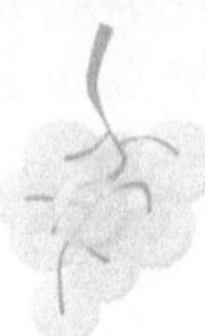

Making peace

*People are always expecting to get peace in heaven; but
you know whatever peace they get there will be ready
made. Whatever making of peace they can be blest for,
must be on earth here.*

John Ruskin, The Eagle's Nest

Being peacemakers

Jesus said that peacemakers would be blessed and called
children of God. If peacemakers are children of God then
this tells us that God is a peacemaker and his desire is for
peace.

It might not be obvious but his aim is to bring peace to the
world – and when the Spirit works within us he produc-
es peace. But how can we make peace? Can we solve the
problems of the Middle East, change the hearts and minds of
terrorists, turn North Korea away from its nuclear ambitions?
Probably not, at least not on our own.

But like many aspects of the kingdom of God, peace isn't all
about us making grand gestures and achieving impossible
things. The kingdom of God often grows slowly and silently,
and its spreading of peace is no exception. If we're growing
in inner peace and the desire to bring reconciliation, we have
the capacity to spread that peace wherever we go.

We might be able to mediate between colleagues at work or
between family members.

We might be able to defuse a tense situation with a smile, a
kind word, a suggestion of a different way forward or even
just a break for a walk.

We can refuse to take part in destructive gossip, refrain from saying spiteful things, let the aggressive driver go past without retaliation.

We can do our bit to spread a little peace in our corner of the world, to stop being part of the problem and end the cycle of revenge and retaliation which robs us all of peace.

Revenge and retaliation

A woman tells the story of how she tried to get revenge for being bullied as a child with acts of retaliation in her adult life every time she felt wronged. She spread false rumours about her ex-boyfriend cheating on his new partner that led to them breaking up. When working in a bar she overcharged customers who she felt didn't treat her with enough respect.

There were other acts, some big and some small, but the thinking behind them was that they would make her feel better and get rid of her (justified) anger towards her childhood bullies.

But it didn't work.

She just began to find the feeling of power she got out of paying others back addictive and wanted to do more and more hurtful things. And her anger didn't decrease – instead it grew until she realised it was only hurting her and she began to break the cycle and turn to finding ways of working towards forgiveness and peace.

When the Bible said 'an eye for an eye' (Exodus 21.24) its aim was to limit revenge in a time when you could legitimately kill someone for wounding you.

And Jesus extended this limiting of violence further when he told us to turn the other cheek, not to make us doormats but because meeting violence with violence only continues the cycle and we need to find a way to break out of it. And because,

> *The ultimate weakness of violence is that it is a descending spiral, begetting the very thing it seeks to destroy. Instead of diminishing evil, it multiplies it. Through violence you may murder the liar, but you cannot murder the lie, nor establish the truth. Through violence you may murder the hater, but you do not murder hate. In fact violence merely increases hate. So it goes. Returning violence for violence multiplies violence, adding deeper darkness to a night already devoid of stars. Darkness cannot drive out darkness, only light can do that. Hate cannot drive out hate, only love can do that.*

> *Martin Luther King*

Modelling peace

We need to model a new way of being which doesn't focus on getting our own back but works for peace wherever possible. And we need to spend time with God in prayer and contemplation and fill ourselves with the peace that he gives us and which can't be taken away, however much the world shakes around us, so that we begin to radiate that peace to all around us.

This may melt some hearts, and cause people to stop and rethink their words, thoughts and actions. We might not see the effects straightaway, or even at all, and maybe this seems small to us in the face of so much violence, but it might make all the difference in one person's life and in the lives of the other people they meet, live and work with.

What if that aggressive person spoiling for a fight doesn't get you to lose your temper, shout or throw a punch, and recognises that in your refusal to give him the reaction he's hoping for you're behaving much better than him?

Might he have a flicker of guilt, a hint of understanding that he's being unreasonable and maybe even acting dangerously?

Might he take a step back, resolve to get help, find a way to resolve things more calmly, interact more positively with his family and friends?

The ripples of our lives and actions may go further than we imagine. We can't end violence with violence, or hatred with hatred – this only sends us into a never-ending spiral of worsening situations.

God's way of meeting violence and hatred with an offer of peace and love may seem ineffective and even naïve – but we know that God triumphed on the cross not by meeting evil on its own terms but by meeting evil on his terms of love, forgiveness and peace.

We may not be able to sort out the Middle East, and some will call us unrealistic or laugh at the idea that our little bit of peace in our corner of the world will make any difference. But God will call us his children and there will be just a little bit more light and hope in our sad and troubled world.

Suggestions for exploration and prayer

- Are there situations and people in your own life that need more peace? Can you build bridges with others (without putting yourself in harmful situations)? Are there people and situations you need to let go of in order to increase your inner peace?

- Consider whether you could do something to promote

peace, whether it's donating to charity, volunteering, writing to your MP or simply being a voice of reason in a conflict between people you know.

• Draw or find a picture of a drystone wall. On or around the stones write words or phrases which come to mind related to peace and peace making. Use these as prompts for prayer. You could also do something similar with real stones.

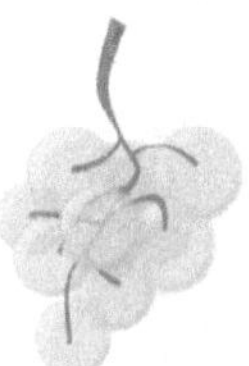

Self-control

Self-control in the Bible

Running the race

The apostle Paul gives us a well-known picture of how self-control can help us when he says:

Do you not know that in a race the runners all compete, but only one receives the prize? Run in such a way that you may win it. Athletes exercise self-control in all things; they do it to receive a perishable garland, but we an imperishable one.

1 Corinthians 9.24-25(NRSVA)

Paul gives us here a picture of an athlete working hard, putting aside temptations to take it easy and find excuses not to train. This athlete controls herself in order to reach her ultimate goal because she knows it's the most important thing in the world. She ignores distractions, keeps away from temptations, and focuses on what she wants to achieve and why. This picture also shows us some important things about how self-control is described in the Bible.

Positive goals

Firstly, self-control isn't about stopping you from doing fun things just for the sake of it or about being a killjoy. Rather, self-control is meant to be about achieving a positive goal.

For an athlete it's a medal, a new personal best or breaking a record.

For a composer it might be producing a symphony or writing a musical.

For a student it might be getting to the end of a degree so that they can get the job of their dreams.

Or it might be about not drinking or cutting down on over-eating with the aim of leading a healthier life.

In this passage, for Paul, the aim of self-control is to help him proclaim and live out the gospel and to be a committed follower of Christ. Thus, he keeps his eye on the prize, remembers his motivation, and doesn't let anything stop him moving towards the goal. And self-control is a tool for getting where he needs to be – closer to God.

Discipline

Secondly, self-control is about discipline.

Discipline here isn't about punishment or correction. In fact the word comes from the Latin for instruction or knowledge and has the same root as the word 'disciple'. It's about learning and following instructions. And learning works best when it's done regularly and consistently. To reach our positive goals we sometimes need discipline.

We sometimes need to make sure we regularly carve out time to do the things necessary to reach our goals – and for a Christian this might mean making sure we regularly set time aside for prayer, Bible reading and worshipping God and don't let other things get in the way of that. Then we can learn more about God, draw closer to him and find our way along the path he's laid out for us with growing confidence, skill and understanding.

Focus

Thirdly, self-control involves focus.

We need to make sure we stay committed to goals, and we need to use discipline to commit ourselves to working towards them. But focus is also a limited resource. We can only focus on so many things at once, and if we surround ourselves with too many distractions, or even well-meaning goals, we can end up not being able to do anything. It's like when we make New Year's resolutions and end up with a list that we have no hope of keeping because there are too many things to do at once.

The secret to achieving goals is not to have too many, to break them down into steps, and to focus on what's most important to us. So, we need to know what is important for us to focus on at any one time and stick to that, not letting ourselves get overwhelmed with trying to do too many things at once or letting distractions pull us away for our aim.

However, we do also need to remember that focus can be unhealthy if it tips over into obsession and we become someone who can't see past a single issue, aim or idea to the wider world.

Sometimes we just need to relax and have a break, so we can be refreshed and renewed and avoid becoming one-track minded people. And we need to remember that other people also need our attention and care – it's not all about what we want to achieve. What might seem to us to be an interruption or detour on our path may in fact be a vital task given to us by God.

The whole person

Self-control is something that needs to be a characteristic of our whole selves. It's hard to control what we do or say if we aren't able to control our thoughts. If you've ever come across cognitive behavioural therapy (CBT) you'll know that it works on the basis that how we think affects our emotions and in turn our actions. So, if we think that everyone hates us we'll feel sad or angry and avoid other people.

But if we think that actually some people like us and some

people don't then we are more likely to go out and try to engage with others – and take it less personally if people don't always respond positively.

There is a similar idea here. If we control how we think about other people, then how we behave towards them will change. If we avoid thinking of ourselves as better than everyone else then we'll be less arrogant and this will affect how we act. And if we also avoid going too far the other way and thinking we are rubbish then we'll be more confident about offering what we can to other people.

How we think affects what we do and how we feel, so controlling our thoughts is vital for not letting our emotions run away with us and for determining how we act.

Suggestions for exploration and prayer

- Consider, perhaps in a journal, what goals you have or would like to have, and how you could help yourself stay motivated enough to stick to them despite distractions. Write down what you'll need to do to achieve your goals, what you might have to do less of to achieve them, and how they will help you be a happier, healthier person in body, mind or spirit.

- If your habits of thought are affecting your emotions and actions think about whether something like CBT might help. You can see a therapist or find many helpful books and online resources for this.

- If you are troubled by feeling that there are areas in which you lack self-control, try writing these down in a prayer to God and pinning them to a cross as a sign of giving them over to God and receiving his help and forgiveness.

The helpfulness of self-control

Lacking self-control

Imagine a small child having a tantrum – complete with throwing toys and screaming – when he doesn't get what he wants. This isn't unusual for a small child, of course, but imagine that this child doesn't grow out of it and that he isn't taught a better way of reacting to frustration.

Imagine that the child doesn't learn self-control.

Perhaps he doesn't do well at school because he gives in to the urge to play games on the computer instead of getting down to homework.

Maybe he finds it hard to make friends because he can't share or stop himself shouting or sulking when things don't go his way.

Twenty years later the man that this child has become shouts in the face of his boss when he's asked to do something he doesn't like – and promptly loses his job. Or he constantly sulks and is manipulative and demanding when his partner doesn't do what he wants, instead of being willing to converse reasonably and make compromises, and the relationship ends.

Imagine that he constantly makes unreasonable demands on the people around him, expecting them to do everything he wants and giving them little in return. Eventually he'll drive them away. He might also refuse to put the effort in to do things properly, making his life more difficult in the long run as things fall apart or have to be redone. He might not learn to rein in destructive impulses but instead puts himself or even others in danger with reckless behaviour.

We all know what it looks like to lack self-control. People who lack self-control have tantrums or sulk when they don't get their own way. They are often unable to stop doing things which cause them or others serious harm. And they lose jobs, friendships, marriages and respect because they can't control their reactions or learn how best to respond when things don't go their way.

Reaction or response

The main thing self-control does is help us decide how we will respond to things. It frees us from just reacting blindly based on a fleeting emotion or instinct or because it's what we've always done.

Maybe as a child you were advised to count to ten before reacting to something that had angered or upset you. That is self-control in action, giving you a breathing space to calm your first urge to lash out, run away or do something else that you might regret.

For self-control enables us to respond rather than react, to choose what we will do or say, to make a wise choice and to act reasonably, rather than just reacting in the heat of the moment in a way that might not serve us or others well.

Self-control frees us from being swayed by every passing thought or emotion and puts us more in control of our lives by giving us the ability to choose what we do or say. It helps us think about whether it really is a good idea to shout at our boss, to try to manipulate our partner, take up all our friends' time with unreasonable demands or to try to force the world to give us everything we want at the exact moment we want it. It helps us decide whether we really want to do things that might make us feel better in the short-term but are actually bad for our health, like smoking or drinking too much.

And, as we use self-control to help us make good decisions about how we relate to others, we display love for our neighbour in action as we take the time to think about how we should respond as children of God dealing with our brothers and sisters.

We avoid screaming at people and instead find ways to discuss things calmly and find solutions to problems.

We don't insist on having everything our own way but instead recognise other people's needs and wants as being important.

We give other people the space and time they need to flourish and grow by not imposing our will on them or riding right over them.

Such things help us build better, deeper and longer-lasting relationships, which in turn makes us happier and more fulfilled. And in developing the ability to focus on what's important and worth thinking about we develop our capacity to avoid letting fleeting distractions get between us and God.

Perseverance and success

Another positive outcome of self-control is that it helps us to persevere and, in preserving, we're more likely to reach our goals. (Perseverance is also an important part of patience which I'll talk about later in this book.)

Perseverance depends on having the ability to keep working when we'd rather watch TV, to put up with boredom instead of demanding distraction, and to not give up and go off in a huff when things don't go our way.

A musician becomes successful by having the self-control to practice every day, including the boring bits like scales.

A sportsperson succeeds by making the right choices about food, by going out and exercising in all weathers, and by ignoring the impulse to claim they are too tired.

Success in these and many other areas depends on us having the self-control to ignore distractions, not give in to the urge for instant gratification, and to instead persevere towards our goals, for without self-control we're likely to decide that something difficult isn't worth doing. We are likely to think that everything should always go our way and to get angry and blame everyone and everything but ourselves when they don't, instead of finding out how we can try to make things better.

But with self-control we can find the resources we need to carry on – in our daily lives, in our relationships and in our walk with God.

Suggestions for exploration and prayer

- Using a self-control spinner can help us regain control when our feelings seem to be running away with us. Find a CD or DVD and decorate it any way you like. Put some Blu Tack (or similar) over the hole in the middle and spread it out a bit around the sides, then push a marble into it. If you want to create more of a handle, put a bottle cap on top of the marble. You can then spin and stop the spinner whenever you like, to remind yourself that you can control your emotions and can ask God for help to do so.

- Learn a verse or two from the Bible related to being self-controlled. You could write one down and put it somewhere you will see it regularly.

- If you feel able to, find a trusted friend or advisor and share with them any particular areas of self-control that you struggle with. They can encourage you, give advice and help you to persevere as God grows this aspect of the fruit of the Spirit in you.

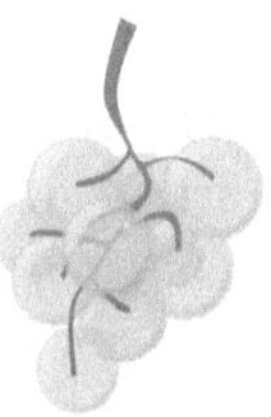

Growing self-control

The social animal

It's one thing to say that we need self-control but how can we grow it?

The journalist David Brooks, from *The New York Times*, wrote a book called *The Social Animal*, published in 2011. This book discussed what drives individual behaviour and decision-making, drawing on psychology, sociology and biology. The book has been commercially successful, although it received mixed reviews from experts, but what we are concerned with here is one particular thing that Brooks pointed out.

He noted that some experts have claimed that to change unhelpful or negative behaviour you just have to point out the long-term risks. By way of example he says:

> *Smoking can lead to cancer. Adultery destroys families, and lying destroys trust. The assumption was that once you reminded people of the foolishness of their behavior, they would be motivated to stop.*
>
> *David Brooks, The Social Animal*

Yet we all know about people who smoke anyway, have affairs anyway, and lie anyway, with full knowledge of what might happen.

Just knowing that something is a bad idea which will have bad consequences won't necessarily stop people doing it. And the reason for this is that our brains tend to treat our future self as a stranger.

When we imagine ourselves in the future our brains often

start thinking as if we're imagining a completely different person who we don't know and don't really care much about. This means that whatever the future consequences of our actions might be there is a tendency to think as if they'll happen to someone else – and not even someone important.

And the more inclined our brains are towards thinking in this way, towards seeing our future self as a stranger, the less likely we are to show self-control and make choices that help other people.

Previously in this book (in the section called 'The two thieves') I talked about the importance of not living too much in the future as this can rob us of our joy. But as so often in life we need balance – here, between living in the moment and thinking about the future.

It's not helpful to spend so much time looking forward to the future that we forget to live now but sometimes we do need to think about the future consequences of how we live and consider where we're going, how we might get there, and whether we really do want to go in that direction.

Going back to Brooks, it's a strange quirk of our psychology that we tend to see our future selves as strangers but it explains why people know all about why they shouldn't keep doing something but carry on – it takes a conscious effort to realise that twenty years down the line it might be us with lung cancer and not an imaginary stranger.

So, Brooks continues:

> *Both reason and will are obviously important in making moral decisions and exercising self-control. But neither of these character models has proven very effective.*
>
> *David Brooks, The Social Animal*

In other words, just knowing what we should do isn't enough to change our behaviour. We need something more to motivate us to change. So, what can we do?

Getting help

Well, firstly, we're not controlled by our biology.

It may incline us towards a particular way of thinking and doing things but as human beings we can choose to be aware of our biases and do things differently. And it's not the case that we can't think about ourselves in the future at all – otherwise no one would ever change for the better, and there are plenty of ex-smokers and other people who've changed their behaviour to prove that this isn't the case.

What we need to do if we want to grow in self-control is not just know what we want to change but find something that'll help us to recognise what we are doing, its consequences for us and those around us, and help us to change.

Other people can help us with this, through inspiring examples or wise advice. And sometimes circumstances force an urgent need for change onto us, such as if we become ill or a relationship breaks down.

But the best source of the help we need is God.

The fruit of the Spirit is something that is grown in us by the power of the Holy Spirit. It's not meant to be something we grow all by ourselves. It involves God's power at work in us to help us change and grow to become more like Jesus as we open ourselves to his influence and cooperate with the Spirit's movement in our lives.

And if we really want to be transformed by the Sprit's power then this means making sure we abide in Christ, becoming one with him and drawing on his power to change and heal:

Abide in me as I abide in you. Just as the branch cannot bear fruit by itself unless it abides in the vine, neither can you unless you abide in me. I am the vine, you are the branches. Those who abide in me and I in them bear much fruit, because apart from me you can do nothing.

John 15.4-5 (NRSVA)

In these words from John's Gospel we see our need of Jesus to give us the power and ability to change, flourish and produce fruit. Like branches that can't survive without their stem, let alone bear leaves and fruit, we need Jesus in us in order to live and grow. We need to depend on God to keep living and growing and doing good things. And we see that Christ sustains us, makes our growth possible and is the source of change and growth in our lives.

So, if we want to grow self-control we may need to remember and try to overcome our bias towards thinking that consequences won't happen to us. We may need to become more conscious of the areas where we have weaknesses and resist the temptation to give in to anger, over-indulgence, or whatever our particular difficulty may be.

But, ultimately, our ability to grow self-control comes from being rooted in Christ through prayer, worship, Bible study and Christian fellowship, with an openness to the Sprit and a willingness to allow him to transform us as he grows his fruit within us.

Suggestions for exploration and prayer

• Is there someone that you admire and find inspiring because of the way they have grown in faith and love? This might be someone personally known to you or a well-known person from the past or present. Think about what you admire in them and see if you can find out something about how they have become that person and whether they have had to exercise self-control.

- Find ways to make sure you keep spending time with God, in whatever ways help you to draw close to him, and persevere in prayer, worship and Bible reading. You can find a long list of different ways to connect with God depending on your natural tendencies and preferences at https://onethingalone.com/ultimate-list-creative-ways-connect-god-120-ideas/ or there are many other books and resources available for exploring this.

- Try to stay aware of the tendency to think that our future self has nothing to do with us and try to develop the habit of thinking about how constantly making impulsive and unhelpful decisions might harm us or others down the line.

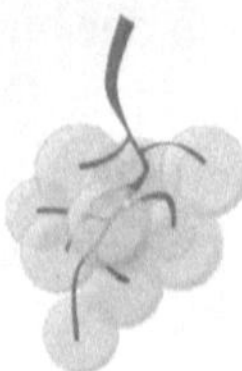

PATIENCE, GENTLENESS AND FAITHFULNESS

Patience, gentleness and faithfulness deal with how we treat one another.

Patience is an outward sign of our love for one another, and of our ability to exercise control over our reactions in a way that helps to build each other up.

> *I therefore, the prisoner in the Lord, beg you to lead a life worthy of the calling to which you have been called, with all humility and gentleness, with patience, bearing with one another in love, making every effort to maintain the unity of the Spirit in the bond of peace.*
>
> *Ephesians 4.1-3 (NRSVA)*

Gentleness teaches us that the way to succeed is not by shouting, roaring and forcing our will on others, even though these are the messages we get from the world around us. Instead, we succeed by holding power under control.

> *But the wisdom from above is first pure, then peaceable, gentle, willing to yield, full of mercy and good fruits, without a trace of partiality or hypocrisy.*
>
> *James 3.17 (NRSVA)*

We need to show faithfulness towards God, of course, but also one another, as a sign of our commitment to living well in community and caring for others.

> *Let each of you look not to your own interests, but to the interests of others.*
>
> *Philippians 2.4 (NRSVA)*

Patience

What is patience?

I wonder what 'patience' means to you. Does it just mean passively sitting around waiting for something to happen to us or for a good thing to come our way? Or is there more to it than that?

Looking at biblical references to patience, there seem to be two different sets of circumstances in which we're called to grow patience.

Working towards our goal

Firstly, there are those verses that talk about patience as an active thing designed to help us reach a goal, something closely related to perseverance. In these verses we're told to keep going in the race:

Therefore, since we are surrounded by so great a cloud of witnesses, let us also lay aside every weight and the sin that clings so closely, and let us run with perseverance the race that is set before us...

Hebrews 12.1 (NRSVA)

We're encouraged to bear fruit through perseverance:

But as for that in the good soil, these are the ones who, when they hear the word, hold it fast in an honest and good heart, and bear fruit with patient endurance.

Luke 8.15 (NRSVA)

To keep doing good while we wait for God:

So let us not grow weary in doing what is right, for we will reap at harvest time, if we do not give up.

Galatians 6.9 (NRSVA)

To wait hopefully:

> *But if we hope for what we do not see, we wait for it with patience.*

> *Romans 8.25 (NRSVA)*

And to not be sluggish:

> *And we want each one of you to show the same diligence, so as to realize the full assurance of hope to the very end, so that you may not become sluggish, but imitators of those who through faith and patience inherit the promises.*

> *Hebrews 6.11-12 (NRSVA)*

There's nothing passive or inactive about these images. Rather they call us to keep on trying, to not be discouraged, and to resist falling into despair and apathy, even though the road is long and sometimes we seem not to be moving at all – or even going backwards.

In much the same way, a musician keeps practising those difficult passages, an athlete keeps trying to beat his or her best time, and we all work to improve at the things we care about and want to do well in, whether at work, home or college. This applies even when we keep falling into sin or meet with setbacks, failures and disappointments. The point here isn't that we must be the best but that we need to just keep going in hope, faith and love through the challenges of life and faith.

When we don't have any answers

In this set of circumstances, the focus is on holding on to God when we can't do anything. This is important when we don't have a plan, don't know where we're going and can't see how things will work out. Sometimes we have to wait for God, for answers, for a solution or a way forward, even if it goes against the grain of wanting to solve everything now, get answers, or to stop all the bad things in the world.

Then we need to:

> *Be still before the* L ORD *, and wait patiently for him…*
>
> *Psalm 37.7 (NRSVA)*

But there are other times when no answer seems to come Moments when we might want to say:

> *My God, my God, why have you forsaken me?*
> *Why are you so far from helping me, from the words of my groaning?*
> *O my God, I cry by day, but you do not answer;*
> *and by night, but find no rest.*
>
> *Psalm 22.1-2 (NRSVA)*

Sometimes we can't fix a relationship.

Sometimes we don't know why we or a loved one is suffering.

Sometimes we lose a job or experience a disaster through no fault of our own and can't immediately see the reason why or what we might be able to do next.

God wants what's best for us but sometimes we don't get an answer to our questions in this life. We may not know why things turn out a particular way or why some things aren't fixed for us but we're called to have faith, patience and trust that the God who loves us will one day put everything right.

Justice will be done, hurts healed, sin, suffering and death done away with, but it's a process that takes time. And sometimes we need to wait because we don't have all the facts, because rushing in might make things worse, or just because we can't force people to see things our way or do things how we would like them done.

Sometimes patience means accepting that we can't control everything. However, this isn't a call to just put up with anything. There are times when a situation is too damaging, dangerous or unsolvable for us to keep throwing ourselves endlessly into it. At these times the best solution may be to walk away for I don't believe that God wants anybody to destroy themselves trying to resolve an impossible situation. Instead we can show patience in living with an unresolved situation, leaving it to God to sort out in his own time and way, whether that's in this life or the next.

Patience in all circumstances

So patience is needed in two sets of circumstances. One is when we need to keep going with active efforts to live out our faith in our lives and make things better. The other is the difficult task of holding on to God even when we might not see any results. Both can be tricky to do but we're not alone. We always have the help of the Spirit, guiding us and growing the fruit of patience within us.

Suggestions for exploration and prayer

- Consider whether there are situations that you are impatient with or which you are continuing in when it would be best to walk away. Ask God for wisdom to know the best thing to do in these circumstances and courage to live with things that can't be resolved.

- Using a journal might help you see the ways in which changes are happening that are too slow to see in the rush of daily life. It doesn't have to be a written journal – pictures, music and objects can all be used.

- Meditation can help us to develop patience and bring our focus back to what is really important out of all the things that might cause us impatience.

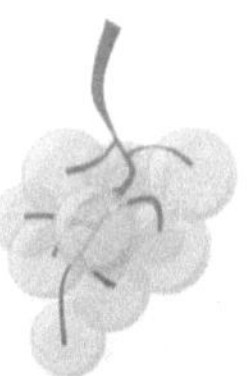

Keep on keeping on

Patience and perseverance

The first person to cross the English Channel in an aeroplane was Louis Blériot. But he only achieved this through perseverance. He built and wrecked ten aeroplanes until, on the 25th July 1909, he finally made it across in his 11th machine – and even then it was with an injured foot.

I mentioned before that patience can be closely related to perseverance. I've been watching a programme on TV in which a young girl goes straight from never having played a sport in her life to instantly being considered for a top team. It gives the impression that we can get what we want instantly rather than that to be a good sportswoman (or artist, writer, mechanic, gardener, cook or anything else) you need patience.

Patience means spending years practising, training, learning, studying, failing and trying again.

Patience means not giving up, taking the easy way out or just going on to something else when it gets boring or difficult.

Patience means recognising that the best things in life need time and will be rewarding if we stick at them.

Patience is often underrated as we're encouraged to believe that if we follow our passion, believe in ourselves and dream big we can always get what we want when we want it.

Focusing on what inspires us, doing good things that we enjoy and not shrinking away from life out of fear are all positive. However, we run the risk of almost expecting the universe to arrange itself so that good things fall into our laps with little effort or waiting on our part. We want it all to happen now, and we forget that great things are achieved by perseverance, by grasping what we want to achieve, by holding on to it, and by not letting go.

The kingdom way

Doling everything out immediately is also not the way of the kingdom of God. That's not the way things work and neither is it very healthy for us human beings.

We live in a culture of instant gratification, where we can get almost everything straightaway and so we become ever more demanding. As an example, I remember as a child when you would sometimes have to save up coupons for some kind of prize, send them off and then wait six to eight weeks to get it. Now, we have overnight deliveries from Amazon. But we also have more stress, more impatience, and more irritation when things don't go our way instantly.

In Scripture God's kingdom is compared with slow things that start small and work unseen, like yeast and mustard seeds. God can work suddenly and loudly but is more likely to gently and quietly build and produce and encourage, year by year, never giving up but unwilling to push us beyond our limits.

This can seem frustrating but it's in the nature of things that maturity takes time, and we need patience to master new skills. Children need patience to learn skills like tying their shoelaces, reading, writing and maths, as well as the skills of sharing, being friends and dealing with conflict. And parents and teachers need patience to help children learn and develop at the right time and in the right way.

And we need patience later in our lives. It takes time to learn how to drive a car, work out a budget, know how to do well at work, run a house.

God works tirelessly to bring about his purposes and restore all things to how they should be, little by little, with infinite patience. He works to bring things to maturity, to fullness and ripeness in the right way and at the right time. It's not that God is doing nothing, or that he hasn't got round to starting yet. He is always working and we're waiting for the fullness of his work to be revealed. Not in an aimless way but in the same way as a gardener waits for seeds to sprout, a pregnant woman waits for her child to be born or a writer waits for an idea to form.

As Paul says:

> *I am confident of this, that the one who began a good work among you will bring it to completion by the day of Jesus Christ.*

> *Philippians 1.6 (NRSVA)*

If this is what God is like, patient and persevering, then as his creatures, created in his image, it makes sense that this is a good way for us to be as well.

Yes, we can go after the quick and easy options in life, avoiding things which are hard or take a long time or are sometimes boring, but we risk missing out on so much. We might miss a chance to learn and perfect a skill, discover a talent, find a gift, and the sense of achievement and joy that comes with these things. We could lose opportunities to find real, deep, lasting growth and wisdom in our lives through waiting patiently on God, seeking him through word, prayer, sacrament and the things he calls us to do and be.

Without a sense of patience we might try to rush on ahead, wanting to be transformed now, to have mastered everything now, to get everything right now. But in that rush and anxiety we might miss the small joys and beauties of life, like a laughing child, a singing bird, five minutes quietly sitting and watching the world go by, a chat with a friend. We might forget that the process of changing, learning and becoming is as valuable as the end result.

And we might forget to

> *Be still and know that I am God!*

> *Psalm 46.10 (NRSVA)*

Suggestions for exploration and prayer

- It can be easy to get discouraged and give up when a goal seems a long way off. Then it can be helpful to break that goal into manageable chunks, not looking too far ahead but focusing on what we can do now.

- Sharing wishes, dreams and ambitions with others can help us build a team of people to cheer us on and encourage us to keep going when we feel impatient with our progress.

- Remember to enjoy the small triumphs and joys as you go through life, not just focusing on the end result but enjoying the process and journey. Getting into the habit of being grateful for something every day, however small, is a good way of keeping hope and patience alive.

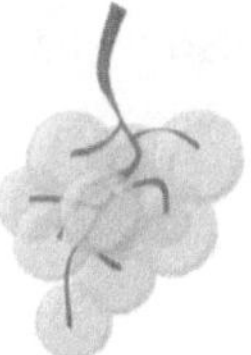

Patience with the annoying

Road rage

A few years ago it was reported that the UK has the highest rate of road rage in the world. This isn't always the really extreme things like physical violence but it does mean that a huge number of British people are getting angry over perceived slights and apparently bad driving by other people. And, of course, we are always much better drivers than everyone else on the road!

In fact, as one person has said,

> *Patience is something you admire in the driver behind you, but not in the one ahead.*

> *Bill McGlashan*

Let's be honest, though, on our overcrowded and pot-hole-filled roads it can be annoying to be stuck in a traffic jam or endless roadworks, or to be behind someone going a little bit slower than we want to go, and it's tempting to let rip from the safety of our motorised boxes. Some are even tempted to act more dangerously – to tailgate or flash their lights, blare their horn, slam on brakes in front of people or even get out of the car and try to start a fight. Thankfully such extreme reactions are rare but anger on the roads is an issue for us all.

I think, though, that it is also just a symptom of a wider problem.

We want it now

In our modern Western world we've become used to the idea that everything should be available immediately, or close to it, with no frustrations or delays. We've gone from the computers of my childhood, where you waited maybe five minutes for a game to load, to computers where if we don't get our game, website or social media page to load in a few seconds we're likely to give up in disgust. We have instant communication, fast food, TV on demand, access to a world of information on the Internet, and sometimes an expectation that whatever we want to have, or do, or be should be available instantly. And this expectation spills out into the rest of our lives, reducing our tolerance for everyday obstacles, slow moments, hesitations and hindrances.

Social media

Through social media we can also surround ourselves with people who think like we do and respond with outrage to anyone who challenges us.

We run the risk of forgetting that we're dealing with real people, who may have good reasons for their opinions, even if we don't like them. And because we forget, we start lashing out, calling people names, attacking them in a way we would never do if we were face to face. We may even become 'keyboard warriors' – people who use the anonymity of the Internet to make abusive and aggressive comments.

There was a situation once where I made a comment online which someone jumped on and attacked but I had a chance to talk privately to the person behind it and we ended up actually understanding each other and parting on friendly terms.

Of course, sometimes people need to be called out for their words or behaviour but how often are we angry because someone's hit a cherished belief or longstanding sore spot or just because we're in a bad mood that day and want someone to take it out on?

Do more, do it faster

There's also increasing pressure at work to work longer hours, get things done faster, and rise up the career ladder ahead of everyone else, filling our lives with more stress and stretching our ability to cope, and our patience ever thinner. And I think the ever-increasing speed of life, the desire that everything should be made as easy as possible, and the increasingly unreasonable demands on our time and energy are having an effect. They reduce our ability to be patient not only with technology or about getting what we want but also our ability to be patient with people around us who may be old or frail or just generally in need of more time.

When people need more time

When we expect our lives to be smooth and free of obstacles that will slow us down, how patient are we with people who might be a bit harder to get to know, who might have strange habits and disagreeable characteristics or who persist in disagreeing with us?

How patient are we with people who need a bit of time to explain themselves or who can't move as fast as we'd like or who just don't understand what we're trying to say to them?

In our rush to get from A to B are we even aware that the people we shout at from our cars might be ill, worried, upset, old or anxious about driving?

Do we remember that our tiredness, stress, anxiety, pressure or general bad day aren't the fault of the person behind the supermarket checkout or do we huff and puff if he or she doesn't scan our shopping fast enough?

As we increasingly interact from behind screens do we forget that the people around us are just that – living, breathing, flawed human beings like us, deserving of our respect, consideration and patience?

Modern life has many stresses, and we all have bad days, but perhaps we all need to stop, breathe and slow down from time to time, and make sure we're extending a little time, space and patience to the people around us. Don't let the pressure to move faster and get more done, along with unreasonably high expectations about getting everything we want straightaway, rob us of the ability to care for others and put in the time and effort with them that they need.

Suggestions for exploration and prayer

- Make a list of the things that annoy you and stress you out. Knowing what our triggers are helps us to be more prepared to deal with them. Pray about these things and ask for God's help in dealing with them.

- If you are going into a situation where you are likely to get annoyed plan ahead to minimise this. If you are driving at a busy time, leave early so you don't get stressed out by slow drivers or roadworks. If you have to deal with someone who rubs you up the wrong way, try to think of something positive about them and remember that we are all annoying to somebody!

- Remember to breathe! It seems a small thing but taking a moment to take a few deep breaths, maybe saying a small prayer or Bible verse as you do so, can really help to bring down your levels of irritation.

- If you are finding that everything is annoying you then maybe you need a break. Get some sleep, go for a walk, play with a pet, watch a film, go out to a new place. Putting time and distance between you and your stresses can bring a whole new perspective and strength.

Gentleness

The gentleness of God

Power under control

As a child I once had a go at riding a horse. I didn't get very far as I was too nervous and not very well-coordinated but I did learn something about gentleness in the sense meant in our passage from Galatians.

A horse is obviously a large, heavy and powerful animal, weighing up to 1,000 kg or 157 stones, that is capable of doing some serious damage to a small, squishy human being. They also gallop at around 27 miles per hour, so you want to hold on if riding one at speed!

Yet, looking back now, despite my nervousness I have never yet been harmed by a horse. It's possible to walk up to them, stroke them, climb on their backs and get them to go places. Their power and strength are kept under control and used for good purposes. Horses are generally gentle not because they are weak – far from it – but because their strength and power are held in the proper channels.

For gentleness is power under control.

God's power

Many years ago I was in a group of people all doing short talks on a subject of our own choice. I don't remember what most of us talked about, except that one person talked about Canada and I talked about keeping chickens, and the funny things they do sometimes. Then, it was the turn of someone who announced to a room full of people that God could strike us down at any time if he chose.

This is technically true but it certainly caused an uncomfortable silence, coming as it did after a rather cheerful, friendly discussion. Even now I think I would be slightly scared if I met that person again. They weren't wrong, as such. God certainly could do away with this world or the whole universe, impose his will on every living thing, stamp out all argument and disagreement with him by force, and generally behave like the ultimate dictator. God has all the power and strength necessary to do exactly what he likes at any time, and who could stop him?

And some do see God in those terms – as a stern and punishing figure, someone to be feared and appeased because of his great power. Yet God doesn't use his power in order to subdue or frighten or impose his will. Instead, God makes space for his creation to live, breathe, reason, love, hate, act and think freely, to develop and change and create. God restrains his own power to command and control in order to make space for us. God lets us make our own choices, even when they're not the best ones, not standing back out of weakness but out of respect for our free will. We can choose to ignore God or listen to him, follow his ways or take our own path.

And God shows gentleness in his willingness to help us through the consequences of poor decisions, mistakes and weak moments if we turn to him, not by waving a magic wand but by entering into our situations, working through them to redeem them and us, setting us back on the right path.

This is gentleness – not weakness or an inability to act but power kept under control for the sake of freedom and love.

Compassion for weakness

God also shows gentleness in his understanding of our human weaknesses and limitations.

Perhaps the best-known example of this from the Bible

comes from the story of Elijah. Having defeated the prophets of Baal, Elijah flees from the anger of Jezebel and then falls into a pit of depression, asking God to let him die:

> *But he himself went a day's journey into the wilderness, and came and sat down under a solitary broom tree. He asked that he might die: 'It is enough; now, O LORD, take away my life, for I am no better than my ancestors.'*

> *1 Kings 19.4 (NRSVA)*

At this point God could have sent an angel to tell Elijah to pull himself together and get on with his job, to 'man up' as it were. Yet, instead, God sends an angel bearing food and drink, lets Elijah rest for a while, feeds him again and only then sends him on his way. So Elijah goes and meets God on a mountain – not in earthquake, wind or fire but in the sound of silence and God's quiet enquiry about what Elijah is doing there. For although God could have raged and shouted and frightened Elijah into submission, instead he chose gentleness to restore, strengthen and send out his prophet.

Power was kept under control.

And if it hadn't been? If God had berated Elijah – what would've been the result?

For some people in some circumstances that might have worked, I suppose, but Elijah was exhausted, at the end of his resources; the last thing he needed was another blow or show of power for his overwhelmed mind, body and soul. Instead, God's gentleness was the thing that restored him, strengthened him, and made him ready to go out and be a prophet again.

It wasn't a blast of power that Elijah needed but a gentle

hand, for nothing would've been achieved by trying to force him into action when he wasn't capable of it. And it's because we have this gentle and understanding God that we can have confidence. Yes God has power but it's not unrestrained, hurtful power that wants to oppress us. Rather it's power turned to the service of love, to gentleness, to understanding and patient working to redeem, restore and set right: not with brute force but power harnessed and channelled to doing what is helpful, right and good.

Suggestions for exploration and prayer

- Try a breathing prayer to help you experience the gentleness of God. Sit comfortably and as you breathe in imagine the Holy Spirit filling you gently. As you breathe out ask God to take away the things that cause hardness in you.

- Look into a mirror, without vanity, false modesty or harsh criticism of yourself. Ask God to show you how he sees you and understands you as a unique human being who he loves and wants to help.

- Bake or buy some heart-shaped biscuits. Decorate them with icing or anything else you can find in ways that represent gentleness to you. As you eat them pray that God will reveal his gentleness to you or give them to someone else who needs to know about his gentleness.

What gentleness is not

Weakness

If you ever go on YouTube you might have seen one of those videos where people put together clips of people performing acts of kindness towards animals in distress or vulnerable people. These videos often show the most unlikely people taking the time to help a person or animal.

We might see a banker helping ducklings get down from a ledge safely, a group of rough-looking men pulling a dog out of a well, a biker getting a tin can off a cat's head or a white van driver stopping all the traffic on a busy road so that a frail elderly person can cross safely.

These videos are designed to make our lives a bit happier and remind us that there is kindness and goodness in the world. But I think they also show us gentleness. What videos like these have in common is that they show us that you don't have to be weak to be gentle – you just have to care.

Successful business people, those who do heavy physical work and self-employed business-owners all have to be tough in different ways if they are to succeed in their work – and yet they can also show gentleness by taking the time to help someone or something in need.

And often the things that people do in these videos involve a great deal of confidence – if you're stopping all the traffic, for example, you need an inner strength that'll let you get past the fear of being ignored, laughed at or possibly hurt if someone doesn't stop.

And they involve physical strength and the ability to work with others – pulling a dog out of a well needs more than one person: it needs a team of people who are able to work together to use their own strengths in the best possible way.

And they involve being able to see a problem and work out how to solve it – like working out how to get a can off a scared animal's head in a way that won't hurt it, even if the animal is lashing out at you from fear.

Being able to see a situation that needs help, and having the mental and physical abilities needed to do something about it isn't a sign of weakness but of tender strength.

Just a personality trait

Yes some people are naturally more inclined towards gentleness than others but gentleness is also a choice. It's a choice about how we treat others, how we think about them, and how we talk to them.

Gentleness is about showing consideration for other people – their feelings, opinions, needs and preferences, not imposing our own will on others at every opportunity.

Gentleness is about biting our tongue and counting to ten and finding the most helpful response to resolve a problem for everybody – instead of blowing up at every perceived slight or difficulty or using anger to get our own way. This might be direct anger in the form of shouting or a more passive-aggressive approach involving the silent treatment, but both are about forcing people to give us what we want.

Gentleness is about wanting to find ways to make those around us feel loved and cared about instead of aggressively pursuing just our own interests with no regard for what might be best for other people.

Gentleness is about choosing to respond to criticism, attacks or injustice in a gracious way that doesn't just give in to everyone but stands up for truth and justice without resorting to abusive or violent tactics.

Probably the most famous examples of this kind of approach to conflict come from Gandhi in his use of non-violent resistance in the fight for Indian independence, and from Martin Luther King in the civil rights movement in the USA. Neither of these two men just gave way weakly, or put up with things or turned to aggression to get things changed. What they did do was make their points without losing sight of gentleness.

So, gentleness isn't just an aspect of personality that we're born with, like being shy or not shy, but something we can choose to work on and develop, producing this fruit of the Spirit with his help.

About peace at any cost

Gentleness also doesn't mean that we just agree with everyone all the time because we're afraid of conflict.

Neither does it mean just putting up with things that are clearly wrong or using gentleness as an excuse to do nothing.

Gentleness is rather about how we deal with those things that we believe to be wrong, how we approach conflict constructively and how we find a way to make the world a better place.

When someone says something we believe to be wrong, do we jump straight into telling them they're wrong, tell them off for their stupidity or make personal attacks on them? This might be about political opinions, religious beliefs, how to raise children or something as small as the best way to load the dishwasher but, regardless of the cause, lashing out is a common response to differences of opinion.

This is especially true on the Internet, where people often forget that they're talking to other human beings, but it's not the only context where such ungentle responses happen.

Gentleness listens, tries to understand where the other person is coming from, and looks to demonstrate and persuade while showing respect. It doesn't just roll over and give up, letting bad behaviour or harmful words and actions continue, but it finds a more constructive way to deal with conflict by looking for common ground, showing understanding, not getting drawn into unhelpful responses, and being quietly firm about what matters without belittling or forcing people into things.

Overall, we could do worse than remember these words:

Nothing is so strong as gentleness, nothing so gentle as real strength.

Francis de Sales

Suggestions for exploration and prayer

- Get some modelling dough and gently soften it in the warmth of your hands before making it into something that speaks to you of power being kept under control. As you do, reflect on how God gently holds us as he works to gradually change us.

- Maybe find a picture or a poem or story that reminds you of what gentleness is and isn't. Put it up somewhere you can see it often and reflect on it.

• Consider whether there are ways in which you could be gentler or if there are times when you let things go unchallenged when they should be confronted because of mistaken ideas about what gentleness means. Ask God for wisdom and guidance to know how to show true gentleness in your life.

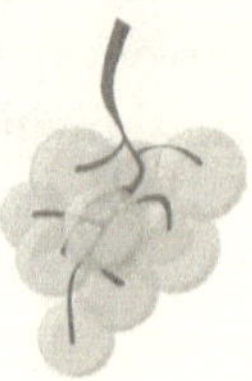

A competitive world

The wind and the sun

The wind and the sun once had an argument in which the wind claimed that he was much stronger than the sun.

He said, 'I'll prove that I'm stronger; see that old man over there with a big coat on? I bet I can get his coat off him much quicker than you can.'

'All right,' said the sun, 'give it a try.'

So, the sun went behind a cloud but left a hole so he could look through and see what happened. The wind blew and blew as hard as he could at the old man, creating a huge storm, but the more he blew the more the old man wrapped his coat around him.

Eventually, the wind had to calm down and give in. Then the sun came out from behind his cloud and smiled down on the old man with his sunshine. After a while the old man began to mop his brow, and then he took off his coat.

And in this way the sun beat the wind.

Competition in business

We live in a world that often seems to value competition over gentleness. People sometimes say things like 'nice guys finish last' and 'it's a dog eat dog world'. This is especially true in business, with its language of competitors and market shares and how much people are 'worth' in financial terms.

Competition isn't always wrong – if it's fair, friendly and ethical it can produce better products and exciting new solutions to problems. It can spur people on to do things better and find ways to contribute something to the world.

But when people are stretched beyond their limits, working long hours to serve the needs of a business that just wants to out-compete everyone else with no concern for its workers' well-being, then competition has gone too far.

When people live in fear of losing their jobs if they make a mistake or don't come up with enough ideas, and when people feel they have to put up with workplace bullying because they fear being considered weak or not up to the job, then competition has become cruel and harsh.

And when people are oppressed with low wages, terrible working conditions and unsafe practices in the interests of lowering prices and increasing profits then competition has been put above human life and above treating people well.

And this isn't God's way.

God's way is to treat workers well and to side with those who are treated badly in their work:

> *Woe to him who builds his house by unrighteousness,*
> *and his upper rooms by injustice;*
> *who makes his neighbours work for nothing,*
> *and does not give them their wages…*

Jeremiah 22.13 (NRSVA)

> *Listen! The wages of the labourers who mowed your fields, which you kept back by fraud, cry out, and the cries of the harvesters have reached the ears of the Lord of hosts.*

James 5.4 (NRSVA)

So, as children of God we mustn't let competition blind us to the need to ensure justice and good treatment of others.

We need to show gentleness by ensuring workers are paid

fairly and don't have to work in poor conditions.

We need to be gentle with the people we work alongside, whether in a paid job or a voluntary capacity, not pushing others to work so hard they become ill, or looking down on people who are struggling, but doing what we can to help.

And above all we need to remember that in everything we do we are ultimately working for God – who hears cries, hates injustice and blesses the vulnerable, the weak and the gentle. For it's not by huffing and puffing that we achieve great things in God's eyes but by knowing how to bring the best out of people and situations with gentle persuasion and care.

Competition in our personal lives

Of course, competition isn't just confined to business or work. It can also exist on a personal level in terms of our abilities, possessions, looks and generally how we think we're doing in our lives compared to everyone else. This kind of competition can be helpful if we are inspired by someone else's example to improve ourselves in a way that enriches our lives. But if it becomes just about getting one over on another person or winning an argument, or trying to prove that we are amazing and everyone else is inferior, then we have a problem. And we have a problem if we let other people's apparent successes convince us we're inferior.

Social media is a particular problem for this as it gives us everyone's edited highlights and almost never people's struggles, insecurities and failures. Not to mention all those 'inspirational' quotes and suggestions that we can do anything if we only try hard enough, leaving us thinking we've failed if we haven't done six impossible things before breakfast.

But this again isn't God's way. God doesn't ask us to strive endlessly to be better than everyone else.

For God is interested in us as we are, and we have no need to prove we're worthy of attention or praise. Yes, God wants us to grow and flourish and bear good fruit. And God wants to help us become more like Jesus. But this is a gentle process that doesn't need to be hurried or completed today.

And we don't need to try to hurry others along either, to insist that they become better in the way we think they should, to win them over to our way of thinking on every issue or to prove that we're better than them. For in the eyes of God we are all his beloved children, all under his care, and,

> *I am confident of this, that the one who began a good work among you will bring it to completion by the day of Jesus Christ.*
>
> *Philippians 1.6 (NRSVA)*

So let us be gentle with ourselves and one another, knowing that we have no need to prove ourselves to God, others or ourselves but resting secure that in God we are loved, valued and helped.

Suggestions for exploration and prayer

- Fairly traded and ethical brands are increasingly popular. You could look into whether you might be able to increase your use of these brands and cut down on buying from companies that exploit workers.

- If you go out to work, paid or voluntary, consider how you can show gentleness towards colleagues and keep harsh or unfair competition in check. If you are more home-based then consider how relationships at home might be too competitive and how you could demonstrate gentleness.

- Take some time to consider how God is working in your life to help you grow as a Christian and a better person. Give thanks for the good work he's doing and ask for help to be gentle with yourself where you still have room to grow.

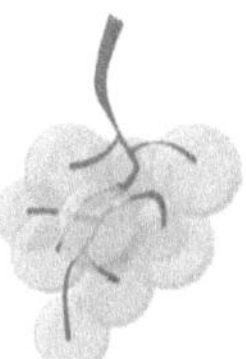

Faithfulness

God's faithfulness

Biblical faithfulness

God's faithfulness is a recurring theme in the Bible.

We see this in God's promise to Abraham and Sarah that they would have many descendants, even though Sarah was well past the age at which she could have children. She gave birth to Isaac, and through him God founded the nation of Israel.

The Israelites were slaves in Egypt for many years but God promised to set them free – and sent Moses to lead them out.

And these are just two examples of the numerous times when God promised to be with his people, rescue them from their enemies, and bring healing and help to those who need it; these promises were kept even when people turned away, failed and doubted God.

Above all, of course, God promised to send a Messiah to rescue us from our fallen nature and sin – and this promise was fulfilled in the coming of Jesus Christ. But these examples are a long way from our ordinary lives here and now, speaking as they do of world-changing events and extraordinary lives.

Ordinary faithfulness

What about those of us who lead more ordinary lives, working in offices, shops or factories, maybe bringing up children, watching TV in the evening, going to the pub at the weekend?

The popular hymn *Great is Thy Faithfulness* may help us here.

Verse 1:

Great is Thy faithfulness, O God my Father;
There is no shadow of turning with Thee,
Thou changest not, Thy compassions they fail not,
As Thou hast been, Thou forever wilt be.

Refrain:

Great is Thy faithfulness!
Great is Thy faithfulness!
Morning by morning new mercies I see
All I have needed Thy hand hath provided
Great is Thy faithfulness, Lord unto me!

Verse 2:

Summer and winter and springtime and harvest,
Sun, moon, and stars in their courses above;
Join with all nature in manifold witness,
To Thy great faithfulness, mercy, and love.

Verse 3:

Pardon for sin and a peace that endureth,
Thine own dear presence to cheer and to guide;
Strength for today, and bright hope for tomorrow
Blessings all mine, with ten thousand beside.

Thomas O. Chisholm

These wonderful words were written in 1925 as a poem by an ordinary person, Thomas Chisholm (1866-1960), as a reflection on his experience of God's faithfulness throughout his life.

Thomas Chisholm was born in Franklin, Kentucky in the USA in a log cabin. He went to a small rural school and became a teacher at the age of 16 before moving into newspapers at the age of 21. He became a Christian in 1893 and then an ordained Methodist minister in 1903. However, he had only a short time in this ministry due to ill health and later became an insurance salesman until his retirement in 1953. While working he wrote poems in his spare time, many of which were published in religious magazines.

In human terms this isn't an earth-shattering life full of wonders, and Thomas had his difficulties and disappointments from his poor childhood to his long-term ill health, as well as the ordinary ups and downs of life that we all face. Yet his poem about God's faithfulness shows that we can see it in both small and large circumstances. The hymn's refrain is based on these words from Lamentations, and shows the constant and reliable faithfulness of God each day of our lives:

> *The steadfast love of the LORD never ceases,*
>   *his mercies never come to an end;*
> *they are new every morning;*
>   *great is your faithfulness.*

> *Lamentations 3.22-23 (NRSVA)*

The first verse of the hymn also reminds us of God's reliability and the fact that we can be sure of his unwavering love and mercy, whatever our circumstances, because God is always true to himself and us. God's faithfulness is based on his unchanging nature as the one who promises and keeps his promises.

Then in the second verse we see how the natural world bears witness to God's faithfulness in its regular and reliable rhythms, its providing of food, water, light and a place for us to live in and delight in. The world that God made reflects his faithful, reliable and constant presence, and without such a world we would find it impossible to live and thrive.

The third verse reminds us of how God has come to us and remains with us through all the joys and sorrows of our lives, however big or small they might be, giving us hope, joy and strength. We can be comforted and encouraged by knowing that our sins are forgiven, that we are loved and understood, that God is with us in our struggles and understands what human life is like. And each day we're supported, helped and blessed by our steadfast God.

Near the end of his life Thomas wrote in a letter:

> *My income has not been large at any time due to impaired health in the earlier years which has followed me on until now. Although I must not fail to record here the unfailing faithfulness of a covenant-keeping God and that He has given me many wonderful displays of His providing care, for which I am filled with astonishing gratefulness.*
>
> *Thomas O. Chisholm*

In this statement we see that God's faithfulness isn't just for kings, patriarchs, prophets and world-changers. It's also for people like us, in all the places where we live, work, play and rest, whatever the circumstances of our lives, and it's a gift on which we can depend.

Suggestions for exploration and prayer

- Jeremiah 29.11 talks about how God has plans to help
  and not to hurt us. Try writing these words down or buy
  a bookmark or similar that has the words written on it
  so that you can keep them with you. Read these words
  through slowly and reflect on them, using them to guide
  you in the things you want to ask God for or give thanks
  for.

- Remember that God hears even our shortest and hastiest
  of prayers. When you feel in need of help or reassurance
  that God is faithful, try shooting up a one-line arrow
  prayer. You could even make some arrow-shaped pieces of
  paper or cardboard in advance and write things down on
  them.

- Take some time to reflect on where God has been faithful
  in your life up to now, looking for his hand at work even
  in difficult times or ordinary struggles, to encourage you
  to trust in his faithfulness.

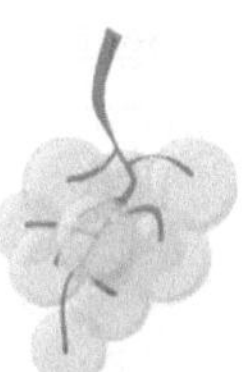

Faithfulness to God

If we have a faithful God, and we want to follow and be like our God, then what can we do? What does it mean to be faithful to God?

Brother Lawrence

One answer may be found in the work of Brother Lawrence (1611–1691). He was born Nicholas Herman in eastern France, wasn't well-educated, and entered the army as a young man in order to escape poverty. During this time he looked at a bare tree in the depths of winter, waiting patiently for new life to grow again. Looking at the tree Nicholas had a realisation of God's grace and providence. Like the tree, he seemed to be dead but God was waiting to give him new life.

Later, Nicholas had to leave the army because of injury and joined a monastery in Paris as Brother Lawrence. He was a popular monk, and visitors came to find wisdom from him, but he wasn't particularly famous in his own time.

It was after he died that the wisdom he'd passed on, in letters and conversations, was put together by the more well-known Abbe Joseph de Beaufort and published as *The Practice of the Presence of God*.

While in the monastery, Brother Lawrence was assigned to kitchen duties, and developed a spirituality of finding God in ordinary things, of being faithful in the washing of pots and pans, the sweeping of floors, the preparing of meals. For Lawrence, faithfulness to God meant doing everything in the awareness of God's presence, of doing the tasks that were in front of him, however ordinary and every day, for the love of God.

He said:

We ought not to be weary of doing little things for the love of God, who regards not the greatness of the work, but the love with which it is performed.

And:

We can do little things for God; I turn the cake that is frying on the pan for love of Him, and that done, if there is nothing else to call me, I prostrate myself in worship before Him, who has given me grace to work; afterwards I rise happier than a king. It is enough for me to pick up but a straw from the ground for the love of God.

Most of us will lead ordinary lives, going to work, maybe raising children, watching TV in the evenings, going to church on Sundays. On the face of it, this doesn't seem an exciting or world-changing way of living. But Lawrence shows us that in everything we do there's the potential to be faithful to God.

Ordinary faithfulness

We can be faithful to God in our jobs by doing our work with awareness of his presence and with a commitment to acting, speaking, thinking and loving as God would have us do.

This means being honest, hard-working, kind and willing to do the boring things with as much faithfulness as we do the interesting ones, and remembering that God is on the factory floor, behind the till in the shop, and sitting in the office just as much as he's in church on Sunday.

We can be faithful to God at home by treating our partners, children, friends and neighbours well, remembering Jesus' command to love others as we love ourselves, and looking for the presence of God among everyone we meet.

We can be faithful to God in our household chores, as well, just as Lawrence was in his, doing them in a way that remembers God's presence with us and offering them as an act of service and love.

We can be faithful to God in how we choose to spend our free time, doing things that are good for our bodies, minds and spirits, that lift us and others up, and which fill us with the joy of drawing closer to God through the things which we enjoy.

We can be faithful to God by using our musical talents, or our skill in communicating either by speaking or writing, by using our talents in art, sculpture or crafts, by baking cakes, doing accounts or helping with administration.

It's not what we do that matters so much when it comes to faithfulness, but how we do it.

God doesn't expect us all to be world-changers, to do amazing things, to be great preachers, evangelists or leaders. What God does ask of us is that we're faithful in our lives and with the things and people he's given us.

What God looks for is people who will remain committed, who can be relied on to play their part, who won't let the entirely human and understandable fear of being different, of looking stupid, of being rejected, stop them living lives that are focused on God and his plans for their lives rather than on what everyone else says, thinks and does.

A prayer

To conclude, there's a prayer attributed to Brother Lawrence which goes like this:

Lord of all pots and pans and things,
since I've no time to be a great saint
by doing lovely things,
or watching late with thee,
or dreaming in the dawnlight,
or storming heaven's gates,
make me a saint by getting meals,
and washing up the plates.
Warm all the kitchen with Thy Love,
and light it with Thy Peace;
forgive me all my worrying,
and make my grumbling cease.
Thou who didst love to give men food,
in room, or by the sea,
accept the service that I do,
I do it unto thee.

Suggestions for exploration and prayer

- Consider the things you do every day and how you do them. Try to be more aware of God as you go about the ordinary tasks of life and consider how you can do them in ways that bring glory to God and help others.

- Do you have talents, skills and abilities that you haven't thought are important to God? Could they in fact be used in his service, even in a small way? Even if your ideas seem a bit off the wall could you give them a go?

- Maybe put the prayer of Brother Lawrence somewhere you can see it and reflect on it, especially if you sometimes feel like you can't do much for God.

Faithfulness to one another

Relationships

Faithfulness is a valued and valuable trait among human beings. Our first thought when we consider faithfulness might be about faithfulness in romantic relationships.

There was once an advertising campaign with the slogan:

The grass is always greener.

This was for a dating agency aimed at married people who wanted to have an affair. The slogan suggests that there is always something or someone newer and more exciting out there. But, when we have made ourselves vulnerable and have built our lives with someone we love and trust, and they betray us, the pain is huge.

It's the subject of many books, plays, songs and films, and its consequences can be far-reaching, affecting the lives of partners, family members and friends. Being unfaithful is a serious threat to any relationship – this is why people who are getting married promise to be faithful to each other for as long as they both shall live. They commit to building a life together based on trust and mutual support.

As has often been said:

The grass is not greener on the other side of the fence – it's greener where we water it.

Yet there is more to faithfulness than not cheating on someone in this way.

Commitment

Faithfulness comes from a combination of what we consider to be important and making a commitment to it. This might be family or friends, our employer, school or college, a sport (whether playing or supporting a team), music, our faith, or even things like a particular brand of car.

Faithfulness is more than just saying such things are important to us; it means acting in ways that demonstrate our commitment.

So we might make spending time with people we love a priority.

We might make sure we work hard for our boss or teachers.

We might practise our sport or music every day, follow our team to matches or attend concerts of our favourite music.

We might make sure we only buy one brand of car.

And we might make sure we spend time in prayer, worship and living out our faith.

These are all signs of faithfulness expressed in a sense that this thing, person, goal is important to us combined with a commitment to the work and loyalty needed to keep them in our lives.

Friendship and loyalty

But if we want to be faithful specifically to other people, to people we know, then what does this look like? One answer is found in the Old English epic poem Beowulf. This is an ancient poem probably passed down for centuries by word of mouth and the earliest written version we have is over a thousand years old. Its themes are universal, though, including the importance of loyalty (faithfulness) to others.

In the poem Beowulf helps Hrothgar, the king of the Danes, whose hall is being attacked by the monster Grendel. Beowulf kills Grendel and then Grendel's mother when she also attacks the hall.

Beowulf is motivated to do this by the fact that many years earlier Hrothgar had helped Beowulf's father in a time of great need, and Beowulf wants to honour that debt by showing loyalty even if it puts him in great danger. In turn, when Beowulf later fights a dragon his example inspires Wiglaf to stand by him when no one else will:

> *Wiglaf was he called ... He saw his lord suffering burning pain under his visor. Then he called to mind the favour that he [Beowulf] had bestowed upon him in days of yore ...Then he could not restrain himself, but gripped the shield with his hand, the yellow wood, and drew forth the old sword ... Then he waded through the slaughter-reek, and bore the war-helmet to the help of his lord...*

> *The Story of Beowulf, Chapter 36*

Beowulf and Wiglaf win this battle but it costs Beowulf his life. However, despite the great danger, Wiglaf doesn't run away – instead he stays close. Beowulf and Wiglaf know that there's much to be afraid of but value friendship and faithfulness more than fear.

This is the faithfulness of true friends and partners: a determination to stick by another person in the bad times as well as in the good. It's a commitment to helping even if it's difficult and dangerous and a practical demonstration of always being there for that person.

We may not be called to be faithful in such dramatic circumstances but there are plenty of opportunities for us to demonstrate faithfulness in our everyday lives. We can all look for ways to avoid being 'swallow friends' – those who stay while summer is here and things are easy but fly away when winter comes and things get hard.

When someone needs help because they've lost their job we can be there to support them in any way we can. When someone is struggling with illness we can offer both practical and emotional help and support. When someone is overwhelmed by the demands of everyday life we can offer to take some of the load, give them a day out or gently suggest some things that might help. When someone's relationship is struggling or broken we can offer non-judgemental listening and care.

And if our friend is sometimes grumpy or non-communicative, has a bad day or has some faults, we don't just disappear at the first sign of difficulty but are committed to trying to work things out and showing mercy and grace where we can. Life has ups and downs, and so do relationships – whether with partners, friends, family members or colleagues.

Yet with faithfulness we can work through many difficulties and come out stronger on the other side.

And, if we have just one faithful person in our life we are blessed – and if we are faithful then we are a blessing to others.

Suggestions for exploration and prayer

- We can all find it difficult sometimes to be a good friend or partner. Ask God to give you wisdom, grace and courage to help others at difficult times. And don't be afraid to ask for help from trusted people when you need help.

- Get or make some heart-shaped pieces of paper and write (or draw if you're feeling artistic) something about a person or situation where you feel that you need to show particular faithfulness to others. Put these somewhere so you can be reminded to do what you can to help and to pray for God's guidance.

- Take some time to remember all the people in your life who have been faithful to you. If you can, tell or show them your gratitude with a note, a gift or an act of appreciation.

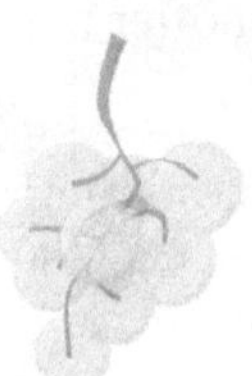

THE FRUIT OF THE SPIRIT

By contrast, the fruit of the Spirit is love, joy, peace, patience, kindness, generosity, faithfulness, gentleness, and self-control. There is no law against such things.

Galatians 5.22-23 (NRSVA)

Working together

I mentioned in the introduction to this book that the fruit of the Spirit is about the positive qualities and characteristics that grow in us as we open ourselves to God's Spirit working in our lives and hearts. It's about God's Spirit working in us to make us more Christ-like and more like the people God meant us to be.

It's not a just a passive thing though, where we just sit back and wait to be changed. Instead, it's something that we co-operate with God in producing. For God won't force change on us that we don't want or aren't ready for – he waits for us to be willing to go with him, to listen to his voice, and to want to be changed.

We might think in terms of someone standing on a ladder picking fruit and dropping it down to a helper below. Unless that helper is ready with a basket and willing to catch the fruit he or she won't get any of it.

And if we want to grow spiritual fruit then we need to be ready to receive what the Sprit wants to give us and develop in us but also to work on helping that fruit grow to its full potential.

In this book we've explored many ways of doing this but the most important thing is to keep the conversation with

God open, to keep seeking after him and his blessings, and to keep going on the journey of faith. This journey won't always be easy or obvious but we can be sure that God holds, supports and understands us, and he will never give up on us.

Intertwined

We can't separate the fruit of the Spirit out too much, saying, well, I'll go for patience but not worry about kindness for now, or I'd like to be kind but I don't want to share so I'll ignore being generous.

For how can we be kind if we're not patient?

And if we're impatient with people then how can we be showing them kindness?

If we don't want to share, and insist on keeping everything for ourselves, how can we show kindness to people in need of what we could give them?

Similarly, how can we have peace without gentleness or gentleness without love?

This is why Paul refers to the *fruit* of the Spirit and not the *fruits*. Because it is one fruit although with many flavours and characteristics.

People who are interested in wine-tasting often talk about the different things they can smell and taste in wines, about the different influences they can detect. They will spend time swirling and sniffing and tasting it slowly to get the full experience of the wine.

Perhaps we could think of the fruit of the Spirit in a similar way – like something not to be gulped down and forgotten but something to be savoured, explored, tested and experienced so that we find out more and more about its depths and subtleties and character. Although we might want to miss out the spitting-out part that wine tasters do!

And the things Paul mentions as making up the fruit of the Spirit – love, joy, peace, patience, kindness, generosity, faithfulness, gentleness, and self-control – together reveal the work of the Spirit within us and how we are growing to be more like Christ.

All the elements of the fruit of the Spirit that Paul mentions in Galatians, and which we've considered in this book, depend on each other, influence each other, and are part of one another. They are things to be explored and experienced together.

For all

The fruit of the Spirit is also something that is for everyone. I mean this in two ways.

Firstly, it's offered to everyone who is willing to open themselves to the work of God within them to transform them. It is the gift of God poured out to all who will receive it. It doesn't depend on us passing an exam or proving ourselves worthy, keeping all the rules or being extra holy. It's just made available to us if we want it and are prepared to receive it and play our part in helping it grow.

Secondly, it's for everyone in the sense that this fruit isn't just to make us feel like we're better people or to give us a sense of being spiritually superior. It's not just designed to patch up our weak points so that we can get into God's kingdom. Rather, this fruit, as well as helping us, is designed to help us to look beyond ourselves and to do our part in bringing in the kingdom of God across the world.

As we bear this fruit it pushes us outwards towards other

people. For if we're filled with love we can't help but want to reach out to others – for love without action is no love at all. We can't be generous or patient without seeing the needs of the people around us and responding to them.

We can't develop self-control without rubbing up against our own and other people's rough edges at home, in workplaces and schools, in our churches and in our communities. Our own peace will spill out into bringing peace to places and people that need it. The fruit of the Spirit encourages us to become people who care about others, who love God and neighbour, and who

> *... love because he first loved us.*
>
> *1 John 4.19 (NRSVA)*

Suggestions for exploration and prayer

- Making a fruit tree can be a good way to remind you of the fruit of the Sprit. You could draw one on cardboard and cut it out, maybe use a picture from a book or magazine, or get some twigs and put them in a container. Cut out some fruit shapes, label each one with an element of the fruit of the Spirit and attach them to your tree. This can remind you of the fruit of the Spirit and help you focus on which area you feel God is leading you to develop.

- You could also gather together different items: pictures, Bible verses or quotes that remind you of different parts of the fruit of the Spirit to help you focus on them and remember them.

- Maybe take some time to write down where you see the fruit in your own life and where you think you could grow some more to help you in prayer and thanksgiving.

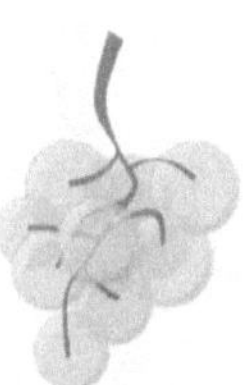

HELPFUL RESOURCES

Books

Below is a list of the most helpful books and other resources I have come across that are mentioned in this book.

Love

Julian of Norwich, *Revelations of Divine Love* (available in various versions and translations)

Isobel de Gruchy, *Making All Things Well: Finding Spiritual Strength with Julian of Norwich* (Canterbury Press, 2012)

Sally Welch, *How to be a Mindful Christian: 40 Simple Spiritual Practices* (Canterbury Press, 2016)

Christopher Chapman, *Seeing in the Dark: Pastoral Perspectives on Suffering from the Christian Spiritual Tradition* (Canterbury Press, 2013)

Kindness

Bernadette Russell, *The Little Book of Kindness* (Orion Spring, 2017)

Generosity

Rowan Williams, *Tokens of Trust: An Introduction to Christian Belief* (Canterbury Press, 2007)

Joy

Arthur Helps, *Companions of my Solitude* (Classic reprint, Forgotten Books, 2018)

C.S. Lewis, *The Screwtape Letters: Letters from a Senior to a Junior Devil* (Signature Classics Edition, William Collins, 2016)

Rob Parsons, *The Wisdom House: Because You Don't Always Have to Learn the Hard Way* (Hodder & Stoughton, 2014)

Peace

John Ruskin, *The Works of John Ruskin: The Eagle's Nest* (Nabu Press, 2009)

Angela Ashwin, *The Book of a Thousand Prayers* (Zondervan, 2002)

Martin Luther King, *Where Do We Go from Here? Chaos or Community* (Beacon Press, 2010)

Faithfulness

Brother Lawrence, *The Practice of the Presence of God* (various versions and translations available)

Self-control

David Brooks, *The Social Animal: A Story of How Success Happens* (Short Books Ltd., 2012)

Exploration and prayer

Some of the ideas mentioned in the book are based on ideas from the following, which you might find helpful if you want to consider different ways of meeting with God:

Claire Daniel, *80 Creative Prayer Ideas* (Bible Reading Fellowship, 2014)

Judith Merrell, *Ultimate Creative Prayer* (Scripture Union, 2008)

Sue Wallace, *Multi-Sensory Church* (Scripture Union 2002)

Sue Wallace, *Multi-Sensory Prayer* (Scripture Union, 2000)

Other resources

John Piper, *Let Your Passion Be Single* quoted on page 62:

https://www.desiringgod.org/messages/let-your-passion-be-single

Greek Poet Hesiod quoted on page 66:
https://www.azquotes.com/quote/669705

Walt Whitman poem, *A Song for Occupations* quoted on page 69:

https://whitmanarchive.org/published/LG/1881/poems/94

Insight Timer – for meditation and contemplative prayer: available from the AppStore and Google Play

One Thing Alone website – lists 120 different ways to connect with God divided into different categories: **https://onethingalone.com/ultimate-list-creative-ways-connect-god-120-ideas/**

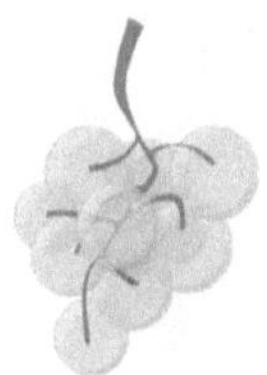

Copyright Acknowledgements

We are grateful for permission to reproduce the following material in this book:

WRF Browning, *Oxford Dictionary of the Bible 2nd edition,* (OUP 2009) © OUP.

Excerpt(s) from THE POWER OF MYTH by Joseph Campbell, with Bill Moyers, edited by Betty Sue Flowers, copyright © 1988 by Apostrophe S Productions, Inc., and Alfred Van der Marck Editions. Used by permission of Doubleday, an imprint of the Knopf Doubleday Publishing Group, a division of Penguin Random House LLC. All rights reserved.

Rowan Williams, *Tokens of Trust: An Introduction to Christian Belief,* (Canterbury Press 2007) © Rowan Williams.

The Screwtape Letters by CS Lewis © copyright CS Lewis Pte Ltd 1942.

Martin Luther King, *Where Do We Go from Here? Chaos or Community.* Reprinted by arrangement with The Heirs to the Estate of Martin Luther King Jr., c/o Writers House as agent for the proprietor New York, NY. Copyright: © 1968 Dr. Martin Luther King, Jr. © renewed 1996 Coretta Scott King.

David Brooks, *The Social Animal: A Story of How Success Happens,* (Short Books Ltd, 2012) © David Brooks

There are instances where we have been unable to trace or contact the copyright holder. If notified the publisher will be pleased to rectify any errors or omissions at the earliest opportunity.

www.ingramcontent.com/pod-product-compliance
Lightning Source LLC
Chambersburg PA
CBHW030933060726
47591CB00005B/1782